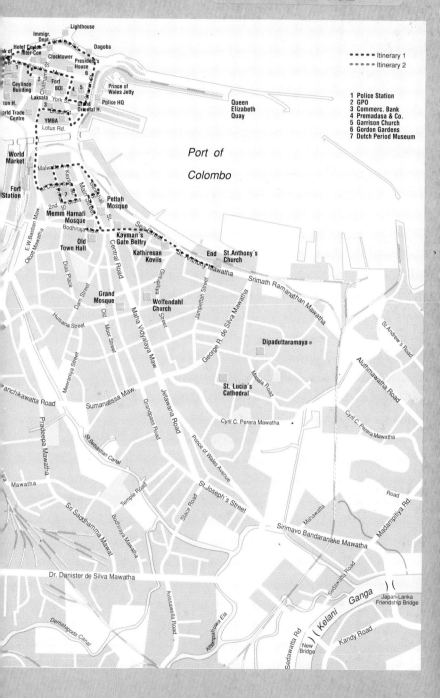

KT-172-702

Legend:
- ●●●● Itinerary 1
- ●●●● Itinerary 2

1 Police Station
2 GPO
3 Commerc. Bank
4 Premadasa & Co.
5 Garrison Church
6 Gordon Gardens
7 Dutch Period Museum

Lighthouse
Immigr. Dept.
Hotel Ceylon Inter-Con
Clocktower
Dagoba
Bank of Ceylon
President's House
Ceylinco Building
Chatham St.
Fort
BOI
Prince of Wales Jetty
Police HQ
Laksala
York St.
Grand Oriental H.
World Trade Centre
Bristol St.
YMBA
Lotus Rd.

Queen Elizabeth Quay

Port of Colombo

World Market

Fort Station

Malwatte Ave.
Keyzer St.
Main Street
Pettah Mosque

Memm Harnafi Mosque
2nd Cross St.
Bodhiraja Maw.

E. W Bastian Maw.
Olcott Mawatha

Old Town Hall
Kayman's Gate Belfry
Central Road
Kathiresan Kovils
Sea Street
St. Anthony's Mawatha
End
St.Anthony's Church

Srimath Ramanathan Mawatha

Dias Place
Dam Street
Grand Mosque
Old Moor Street
Chinupitiya Street
Wolfendahl Church
Jampettah Street
George R. de Silva Mawatha

St. Andrew's Road

Huisana Street
Dipaduttaramaya
Aluthmawatha Road

Meeraniya Street
Maha Vidyalaya Maw.
Masala Road
St. Lucia's Cathedral
Cyril C. Perera Mawatha

anchikawatta Road
Sumanatissa Maw.
Jelawana Road
Grandpass Road
Cyril C. Perera Mawatha
Road

Pradeepa Mawatha
St. Sebastian Canal
Prince of Wales Avenue
Mahawatta
Madampitiya Rd.

Mawatha
Sri Saddhamma Mawat
Temple Road
Bodhiraja Mawatha
Shoe Road
St. Joseph's Street
Sirimavo Bandaranake Mawatha

Dr. Danister de Silva Mawatha

Avissawella Road
Khattampahuwa Ela
Sedawatta Road
Kelani Ganga
Japan-Lanka Friendship Bridge

Dematagoda Canal
New Bridge
Sedawatta Rd
Kandy Road

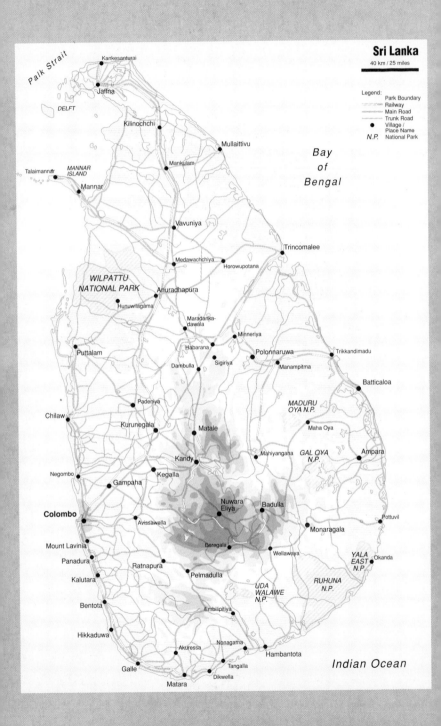

SRI Lanka

Written and Presented by **Vijitha Yapa**

INSIGHT
Pocket
GUIDES

Insight Pocket Guide:

Sri Lanka

Directed by
Hans Höfer

Managing Editor
Francis Dorai

Photography by
Dominic Sansoni and others

Design Concept by
V. Barl

Design by
Laddawan Wong

© 1994 APA Publications (HK) Ltd

All Rights Reserved

Printed in Singapore by
Höfer Press (Pte) Ltd
Fax: 65-8616438

Distributed in the UK & Ireland by
GeoCenter International UK Ltd
The Viables Center, Harrow Way
Basingstoke, Hampshire RG22 4BJ
ISBN: 9-62421-555-3

Worldwide distribution enquiries:
Höfer Communications Pte Ltd
38 Joo Koon Road
Singapore 2262
ISBN: 9-62421-555-3

ayubowan!

Vijitha Yapa

Sri Lanka's literature makes so many references to that first man on earth, Adam, that many believe this island to be the mythical Garden of Eden. Looking around you, it is easy to see why. From the heat of the plains to the cool of the forested hills, from the gem-encrusted hills of Ratnapura to the wide sandy beaches that fringe the island, this is where sea and serendipity, mountain and myth, and rain and religion are all interwoven into one amazing tapestry.

I was born in the deep south and grew up amidst tea, rubber and coconut plantations owned by my father. Having worked as editor of three newspapers in Sri Lanka meant much travel throughout the country. I came to appreciate firsthand, not only the raw beauty of the country, but also the internal conflict and battles the island has suffered.

It is difficult to cram everything I want to show you in this book, so I've selected the best of Sri Lanka for you. Kickstart your holiday with itineraries based in and around Colombo, the teeming capital city where nearly every visitor to Sri Lanka begins his stay. Suggestions on shopping and eating out round off this section on Colombo. Then, embark on a series of excursions to places further afield: to the salubrious hill destinations of Kandy and Nuwara Eliya; to gem-rich Ratnapura; the wide beautiful beaches of the Southern Coast; the untamed beauty of Yala National Park; and the haunting ruins of the northern cities, with tongue-tripping names like Dambulla, Polonnaruwa, Sigiriya and Anuradhapura.

I have trod the paths described in this book many a time and know that you will enjoy your journeys. Savour the diversity and charm of this unique island and you will return again — and again, like thousands of others before you. *Ayubowan — Welcome!*

Contents

Preceding pages: tea estates are a distinctive feature of the island

Following pages: scene from
the Kataragama Festival

HISTORY

The romantics summed up the shape and substance of Sri Lanka when they called it 'The Teardrop of India.' For if the face of the great Indian subcontinent had ever shed a tear of joy, one which froze in mid-air as it fell from her cheek, that teardrop would undoubtedly be the island of Sri Lanka.

To Sri Lankans, this is the original Garden of Eden. They proudly point to places named after Adam – the first man God created – to prove their case. Adam's Peak (7,297ft/2,224m), which the Buddhists believe has the Buddha's footprint, is better known than Pidurutalagala (8,281ft/2,524m), the highest mountain in Sri Lanka. Adam's Peak is one of the holiest mountains in the world, and on a trek to the summit you will find a motley assortment of Buddhist, Hindu, Christian and Muslim pilgrims.

To Muslims, the footprint at the top of the mountain is that of Adam. A narrow stretch of rocks and islands between Sri Lanka and India – all that remains of the land mass which once connected the island to the Indian subcontinent millions of years ago – is be-

lieved to be part of Adam's Bridge. God is said to have broken it into pieces after banishing Adam from the paradisiacal Garden of Eden so that he may never return.

Whatever the veracity of that story, it is the great Hindu epic, the *Ramayana*, which has the earliest reference to the island. Ravana, the 10-headed King of Lanka, seeking to avenge an insult to his sister, travelled to India in a winged carrier called the Dandumonara and abducted Sita, wife of Rama. The enraged Rama enlisted the help of the monkey god, Hanuman, defeated Ravana and reclaimed Sita. Ra-

The venerable Adam's Peak

Culture

vana Ella (Ravana Falls) and Sita Eliya (Sita's Light) in the hill country are associated with that 5,000-year-old story and are visited even today.

Watch out for the peacock-shaped model of the Dandumonara at the turn-off from Colombo's International Airport to the main Katunayake –Colombo road. If you fly the island's national carrier, Airlanka, look out for the logo of the stylised peacock on the tail.

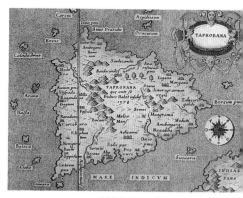

1576 map of Sri Lanka

Serendipity

To Asians, the island has always been called Lanka. But not so to the Arabs or Westerners who braved high seas to visit the land of jewels and spices. Taprobane, Zeilan, Serendib and Ceylon are only a few of the island's plethora of former names.

Etymologists will not be the only ones interested to know that Sri Lanka has contributed to the richness of the English language. The word 'serendipity' – the faculty of making unexpected discoveries by accident – was coined by Horace Walpole in his fairy tale, *The Three Princes of Serendib*. Few people know that the word 'anaconda' (a native South American snake) comes from the Sinhala word, *henakanda*, used to describe a snake with a big body. Strangely, no anacondas have ever been sighted on the island.

Early Origins

According to legend, the Sinhalese people are descended from a lion (*sinha*). This makes the origins of the Sinhala people a fascinating read and brings to mind the story of Romulus and Remus. The *Mahawamsa* (Great Chronicle), the history of the island written by Buddhist monks over centuries and tracing the course of events over 2,500 years, dates the beginning of Sri Lanka's history with the arrival of Prince Vijaya in 544BC. Vijaya, who was to become

Lanka's first king, landed in Lanka from India with 700 followers on the day Lord Buddha died in India. Legend has it that his father, a minor king named Sinhabahu, had been fathered by a lion. This explains the symbol of the lion on the Sri Lankan flag.

Vijaya grew up to be a rebellious young man. When he did not mend his ways despite repeated warnings, his father decided to banish him. Vijaya set sail and landed on a stretch of land in Lanka he called Tambapanni, because of its copper-coloured sand. The *Mahavamsa* recounts that Kuveni, an enchantress and a member of a tribe called the *yaksas*, attempted to bewitch him. Protected by a charmed thread, Vijaya managed to outwit her. He made Kuveni his queen but after a few years, banished her to the forest. Her children became the Veddhas (aborigines), whose descendants even today hunt with bows and arrows.

Buddhist monks, 1883 lithograph

Historical research confirms that the original Indo-Aryan settlers in Lanka were indeed from North India. They mingled with the indigenous races, the *yaksas* and *nagas*, and introduced their Prakit language, which gradually evolved into Sinhalese centuries later.

In the 3rd century BC, the ruler of Sri Lanka, King Devanampiyatissa, embraced Buddhism after a meeting with Venerable Mahinda, the son of the Emperor of India, Ashoka. The capital, Anuradhapura, founded in 437BC, soon underwent a remarkable transformation with Buddhist *dagobas* rising into the sky; incredible feats of engineering which make many marvel even now. Today, Theravada Buddhism is still the primary influence in the lives of the Sinhalese, who form 70 percent of the population.

In 205BC, however, a Tamil warrior, Elara, defeated the Sinhala King and took control of Anuradhapura. It was not until 161BC that King Dutugemunu rallied the people and defeated Elara. Till today, Dutugemunu is the most important national hero among the Sinhalese.

Thuparama Dagoba at Anuradhapura

Invasions Galore

Constant invasions from South India eventually led to the abandoning of Anuradhapura. Over the next few centuries, successive kings shifted their capitals to various cities.

Perhaps the most significant was Polonnaruwa, close to the eastern coast, where the ruins, in a better state of preservation than in Anuradhapura, tell an amazing story of a proud people. Parakramabahu the Great – who ruled the island from Polonnaruwa between 1153 and 1156 – built among other things the Parakramabahu Samudraya, the largest and most spectacular of Sri Lanka's *wewa* or irrigation tanks. Covering 5,928 acres (2,400ha) and a bund with an average height of 40ft (12m), Parakramabahu declared to his people that not one drop of water should pass into the Indian Ocean without it being of some service to man. During his reign, Sri Lanka even exported rice.

When the Portuguese first arrived in 1505, the king was only 8 miles (13km) away at the capital, Kotte, now the site of the present Parliament and the island's new capital. He was told that some visitors who had arrived dressed in iron clothes (armour), ate stones (white bread), drank blood from bottles (wine), and had sticks that made noises like thunder (firearms) were asking for him.

The King ordered the foreigners to be brought to see him but instructed that they be shown a roundabout route so they would not realise how close the kingdom was to Colombo. The enthusiastic guides took weeks to bring in the Portuguese but the game was up when the Commander, who was waiting in Colombo, decided to fire cannons to tell the delegation he was worried by their long absence. The Portuguese realised they had been tricked.

Divide and Rule

To this day, the Sri Lankan expression for taking people for a ride is: 'Like taking the Portuguese to Kotte'. Nevertheless, the Portuguese controlled the maritime provinces until they lost them to the Dutch in 1656. The British replaced the Dutch as rulers in 1796 and it was they who, after plotting with the Prime Minister, finally succeeded in capturing the king in 1815 at Kandy. The island became part of the British Empire. The British introduced coffee into the island but when a disease wiped out the plantations, they turned to tea and rubber.

Universal franchise was first tried out in Sri Lanka in 1931 by the British be-

DS Senanayake

fore being introduced to other Asian lands they ruled. It was not until 1948 that independence was gained, with a parliamentary system of democracy under Prime Minister D S Senanayake. A republican constitution was implemented in 1972 but in 1978 a Presidential system with members of parliament being elected on the proportional system was introduced. The grievances of the minority Tamils erupted in violence in July 1983. This has led to a war in the northern and eastern provinces which continues even today.

Geography

Sri Lanka has a land area of 25,330 sq miles (65,605 sq km) and is about the size of Ireland. Lengthwise it is 270 miles (435km) and measures 140 miles (225km) across the widest point. The population is 17 million with two thirds occupying about one third of the land.

The longest river is the Mahaweli, which snakes its way from the Central Hills to Trincomalee in the east. There, it empties into the Indian Ocean. An ambitious project of successive governments has been to tame the Mahaweli River and perpetuate the legacy of King Parakramabahu not to waste one drop of water. In the 1980s, over US$2 billion was spent to build giant dams to tap the Mahaweli for hydroelectric and irrigation projects, diverting the waters to arid areas to cultivate new land.

The beauty of the island has encouraged tourists to return again and again – and each time discover new things that bind them more. The coastal areas have some of the most beautiful beaches in the world and the chances of anyone feeling crowded on the beach is very remote. There is place and space for everyone in Sri Lanka.

West Coast beach

Historical Highlights

BC

483: Prince Vijaya arrives in Sri Lanka with 700 followers and becomes the island's first King. The dynasty lasts until 1815, with a total of 185 rulers.

380: The island's first capital is established at Anuradhapura.

248: Mahinda, Son of Emperor Ashoka of India, arrives and King Devanampiyatissa converts to the Buddhist faith.

260: Sangamitta, daughter of Ashoka, arrives with a cutting from the bo (*Ficus religiosa*) tree under which the Buddha gained enlightenment in India.

205: A warrior from South India, Elara, captures Anuradhapura and rules for 44 years.

161: Elara is defeated by King Dutugemunu, the greatest national hero of the majority Sinhala community.

AD

993: The Cholas of South India capture Anuradhapura, and the capital is moved to Polonnaruwa.

1070: King Vijayabahu drives out the Cholas.

1505: The Portuguese arrive, build fortresses, extract concessions from the King and begin ousting the Arabs.

1656: The Dutch arrive, oust the Portuguese, introduce Roman Dutch law and begin growing cinnamon commercially.

1796: The British arrive and the Dutch offer little resistance.

1802: Ceylon becomes a crown colony and part of the vast British colonial empire.

1815: The last Sri Lankan King is captured at Kandy after the British plot with his Prime Minister. Lanka's monarchy, which had endured for 24 centuries, comes to an end.

1931: Universal adult franchise is granted.

1948: Ceylon is granted independence on February 4, and D S Senanayake becomes the first Prime Minister.

1956: The ruling United National Party is defeated at the polls and S W R D Bandaranaike becomes Prime Minister.

1959: Bandaranaike is assassinated in September.

1960: His widow, Mrs Sirima Bandaranaike assumes office as the world's first woman Prime Minister.

1972: The name 'Ceylon' is officially changed to Sri Lanka and a republican constitution is adopted.

1978: A new constitution is adopted, with an Executive President at the head and proportional representation introduced. J R Jayewardene becomes the first President.

1987: Indian troops arrive on the island, and later begin fighting with Tamil separatists.

1989: Ranasinghe Premadasa is elected President.

1990: The Indian troops leave.

1993: Exchange controls are relaxed. President Premadasa is assassinated during a rally on May Day. D B Wijetunga is elected President by Parliament.

COLOMBO

As there is only one international airport, everyone arrives at Colombo International Airport (Katunayake) unless they do so by ship or yacht. The ferry between India and Sri Lanka has not been in operation since the early 1980s and the chances of it resuming are very remote due to the fighting in the island's north. The airport is 20 miles (32km) from Colombo and as there is no highway, the length of the journey depends on the time of day one is travelling. It is best to allocate about an hour. Although distances are short, narrow roads coupled with near-maniacal drivers and obstacles like cows, dogs and jay-walkers mean that caution is best.

The Lighthouse Clock Tower

Most flights from the West arrive in the morning while those from the East arrive and leave at night, making travelling easier on the road. But ill-lit roads in some areas makes one wonder whether one is approaching the island's commercial capital or moving away from it!

Because Colombo is a port city, with the sea on the west, the city has expanded more northwards and southwards than eastwards. The main artery is Galle Road, which stretches from Colombo for a distance of 72 miles (116km) to the south to the port city of Galle. Colombo is divided into 15 zones but distances between zones may be short; for instance, it is only about 5 miles (8km) between Colombo 6 and Colombo 7. The main commercial area is the Fort, where the harbour is the dominating feature.

The streets are supposed to have signs in Sinhala, English and Tamil, but often, it may be advisable to look for the names of the roads on shop signboards than on the streets. Some signs can be confusing as they retain old names of roads, leading cynics to say that Sri Lankans do not build new roads; they merely rename roads built by the British with long names. Thus, Parsons Road has been renamed Sir Chittampalam Gardiner Mawatha while Flower Road has become Sir Ernest de Silva Mawatha!

itineraries

A full-day walking itinerary of the city's major sights. Begin this tour from the commercial hub called the Fort – with little evidence of any walls – where historical buildings abound.

Start in the Colombo Fort area where most of the five-star hotels are located. In front of Hotel Marriot is the **Presidential Secretariat**, which was the Parliament until it moved in 1982 to more spacious quarters in the island's new administrative capital, Sri Jayewardenepura Kotte.

No visitors are allowed into the building except on official business. When the President is in his office, there is increased security. A peep through the black grilles reveals statues of recent national heroes, including the first Prime Minister of independent Sri Lanka, D S Senanayake.

Though called the **Fort**, the commercial area of Colombo shows little sign that it was once a military stronghold, defended in turn over centuries by the Dutch, Portuguese and British. In front of the Presidential Secretariat, some old cannons still point out towards the sea, a reminder of the threat of invasion from the ocean in the early days.

Chaitya Road, which hugs the Indian Ocean, is a pleasant walk past the lighthouse on the left, a favourite meeting place for lovers in the evening. Sit on the stone lion and have a photo taken.

Further down is the **Immigration Office** which issues passports. Don't be daunted by the crowds. They are mainly people seeking jobs in the Gulf region who have paid double to collect passports on the same day, often accompanied by friends and relations.

On the left is the imposing *dagoba* (religious monument) which can be seen miles away by those entering Colombo by

Presidential Secretariat

Port of Colombo, a bustling hub

sea. It was built by the port workers of Colombo in 1956 to commemorate the 2,500th year of Buddhism. If you're in the mood for a climb, the *dagoba* is worth a look as an example of modern architecture borrowing elements from the past.

Turn right into Church Street. The **Port of Colombo** lies to the left whilst on the right is the rear of **Gordon Gardens**, now lost forever to the public as it lies within Republic Square in front of the Foreign Ministry. The Gardens contain a rock inscribed with the Portuguese Coat of Arms and a statue of Queen Victoria, both built to commemorate her Jubilee anniversary.

It is a pity that Church Street is closed as straight ahead, past Police Headquarters, lies the **Grand Oriental Hotel**, built in the mid-1850s as barracks for soldiers. The hotel entrance is now via York Street, a detour of about a mile (1.6km). Even the approach road through Chatham Street is now closed because of the Navy Headquarters building. Republic Square, a short cut to the General Post Office, is also closed, all due to security reasons. But take a look at the Grand Oriental anyway, which you will visit later.

Return to the Presidential Secretariat and walk towards the Lighthouse Clock Tower in the distance along Janadhipathi Mawatha. Hotel Ceylon Intercontinental is on the left while on the right is the circular **Bank of Ceylon Headquarters**, which is believed to be tilting. Some say it may one day become Lanka's Leaning Tower of Pisa! The bank has a convenient exchange counter for travellers cheques and cash. In front of the main entrance to the Bank is the **Fort Police Station**, which once housed a Dutch hospital.

Continue walking towards the Clock Tower. **Ceylinco Building**, Sri Lanka's only high-rise building of the 1960s is on the right. Just inside the gate is a little memorial to the last king, Sri Wickrema Rajasinghe, who was imprisoned here by the British after being captured in Kandy in 1815. On the fourth floor of the building is the **Philatelic Bureau** (open on weekdays 9am–3.45pm, Tel: 325588).

YMBA Building

There are sets of Sri Lanka stamps available here, without the long queues at the General Post Office. The **Akasekade Restaurant** is on the top floor from where there is a spectacular view of Colombo.

Where Janadhipathi Mawatha and Chatham Street meet is the **Lighthouse Clock Tower** you have been using as a marker. Probably the best-known landmark of the Fort, the tower built in 1857 is the only lighthouse in the world which also tells the time in the middle of a busy road. Just past it is the **President's House**, where two solitary guards are on sentry duty, one at each gate. The Army, Navy and Airforce take turns in guarding the President every three months.

Opposite this is the colonial **General Post Office** (open 24 hours, all year round, Tel: 326203). There is a special counter for tourists, but as many visitors may want to linger buying stamps as souvenirs, the other lines may be faster.

Janadhipathi Mawatha merges into Sir D B Jayatilleke Mawatha, where **Premadasa & Co** have a gem shop carrying a wide variety of jewellery in beautiful designs. This is also the banking district, where many local and foreign banks have offices. A number of airlines, including Airlanka, are located in this area. The island's Board of Investments has a six-floor building on this street.

At the end, near Seylan Bank, turn left to York Street, where you can change money without much hassle at the Bank of Ceylon's Bureau de Change. At the end of the street is the Grand Oriental

Hotel (GOH), refurbished in 1991 and still retaining its old charm. A visit to the Harbour Room is fun for dinner and to watch the passing ships.

Stroll to the nave of the **Garrison Church of St Peter**, originally the reception and banquet hall of the Dutch Governor's residence. It was first used as a church in 1804. Cross York Street and walk along the shady buildings opposite the Port, and turn right into the extension of D B Jayatilleke Mawatha. There is a good Bata shoe shop where inexpensive shoes are available. On the opposite side, at the **YMBA** Building, are two more shops – DSI and Elasto – which sell locally-made shoes.

Mind how you cross the street. Pedestrian crossings are seldom respected by motorists. The only time Sri Lankans stop for pedestrians is when there is a funeral procession.

The YMBA Building has a lovely Buddhist shrine. A serene Buddha statue beckons those who want a sense of peace and

tranquillity to reflect, even momentarily, on life. The flowers in front of the Buddha are offerings made by the devout. As they make their offerings, Buddhists often utter in *Pali*: 'Gaze upon these beautiful flowers, which in a few hours will wither away. Such is my own life.'

Turn left at Bristol Street and walk to the new headquarters of the Commercial Bank. Nearly touching the walls of the Commercial Bank is the **Delft Gateway**, built during the Dutch period of 1656–1796. The ramparts of the Fort were removed by the British in 1872 to accommodate an administrative building. There were two such gates at one time but no one seems to know what happened to the other.

Return to Jayatilleke Mawatha and cross the road in front of the car park to **Cargills** and **Millers**, neighbouring department stores where the elite of Colombo once shopped. Although run by the same conglomerate today, the stores are a far cry from their former splendour. On the same road is the state-run **Laksala**, excellent for souvenirs of Sri Lanka. Whether it be giant carved masks or coconut shell carvings, a wide range of the island's handicrafts are displayed here in Laksala's spacious surroundings. Across the road is the **World Trade Centre**, opened hastily in December 1991 for the annual meeting of Heads of State of the South Asian Association for Regional Cooperation (SAARC).

Pause for lunch at the **Hilton Hotel** where there is a buffet of Western, Chinese and Sri Lankan specialities for an inexpensive Rs 350. The salad bar is impressive and so are the desserts.

Continue for about five minutes along lower Chatham Street to Olcott Mawatha and encounter Lanka's **World Market**, a day and night bazaar open seven days a week. Here is an exciting array of goods, from leather bags to tee-shirts and toys. No transaction is undertaken without bargaining, so don't pay the first price asked.

Nearby is the **Fort Railway Station**, the main station in Sri Lanka. The train services in Colombo are woefully inadequate, while the outstation services are good but crowded during rush hour. Most destinations have only second and third class coaches, but there is a first class observation coach trip to the hill country which should not be missed.

Opposite the railway station is the outstation state-owned bus depot which serves most parts of the island. Further down the road is the private bus depot. These vehicles take lesser time to reach their destinations because they race through the traffic at breakneck speed. The little streets on the left lead into the heart of the **Pettah**, named from the Tamil word *pettai* and corrupted by the British to Pettah, the old town. Any cross-street leads to the main road and each has developed special characteristics. The first has electrical goods and shoes, the second textiles and clothes, the third hardware, the fourth food items and spices and the fifth wholesale goods and food. Take the first cross-street and turn left to Keyzer Street, which specialises in household items. Turn left again on Keyzer Street to Prince Street, which sells glass, mirrors and electrical items. The old post office in Prince Street is now the **Dutch Period Museum** (open daily 9am–5pm, closed on Wednesday, Tel: 448466), containing some fine examples of furniture.

Continuing along Prince Street, the road joins Malwatte Avenue, the music street selling English, Sinhala and Tamil cassettes. Prices vary from Rs 70–150, depending on the tape length and quality. Sinhala pop is quite rhythmic and Sri Lanka's own *baila* music, with strong Portuguese influences, has a rhythmic style of its own. The lyrics generally poke fun at people and society.

At the Pettah clock tower at the end of Malwatte Avenue in front of Hunters' department store, go down Bankshall Street, the second road from the left. Turn right at the second cross-street to behold the red and white **Pettah Mosque**. It is a pretty sight against the drab adjoining buildings and the minarets look like candy bars. The third cross-street also has the **Memm Harnafi Mosque**, which in contrast is grey in colour and more traditional in architecture.

Turn right on Gasworks Street to see the **Old Town Hall**, restored and now housing shops on either side. In the centre is a large hall. Adjoining it is the **Colombo Municipal Council Museum**, where among the more interesting exhibits are Sri Lanka's first printing machine (by Harrild & Sons of Fleet Works, London), drinking fountains and road rollers. The monument which stood on Galle Face Green, bequeathing the promenade built in 1856 by Governor Henry Ward, also lies in the museum.

We retrace our steps to the main road and turn left to **Kayman's Gate**. The belfry dates back to the Dutch period and may be the oldest Christian structure extant

Pettah Mosque

in Sri Lanka. The word 'Kayman' comes from the Dutch *cayman* (crocodile) as crocodiles once gathered here to eat the leftovers thrown out from the Fort. The bell was rung to indicate closing time for tipplers drinking at the local taverns.

We continue our journey on **Sea Street**, the road where goldsmiths ply their trade. These shops are popular with Sri Lankans and Indians as most brides-to-be come here to shop for gold jewellery. At the end of Sea Street are two beautiful Hindu temples, the old and new **Kathiresan Kovils**.

There are more temples on Gintupitiya Street to the right. Colourful Hindu deities painted in various colours adorn the tall buildings. Sea Street joins St Anthony's Mawatha, and by the sea stands the famous **Church of St Anthony**, a sanctuary not only for Christians, but those of other faiths seeking solace within its walls.

St Anthony's Feast

Take a taxi or auto-rickshaw back to Fort and your hotel. By now your feet will be aching after the long walk. Take a cool dip in the hotel pool and have a relaxed evening. For dinner, try the **Shogun Restaurant** at the Renaissance Hotel, housed in a large stationary boat on the Beira lake.

2. Southern City Sights

A full-day's drive touring the south of the city. Here, shop at Kollupitiya, visit the Buddhist Gangaramaya, traipse through the greenery in Viharamahadevi Park, study artifacts at the Colombo National Museum, and take in the sight of the impressive BMICH and the Independence Commemoration Hall.

Ride-a-bull

Soon after passing the **Presidential Secretariat** (See *Itinerary 1*), on the left is the statue of S W R D Bandaranaike, where we begin this tour.

Prime Minister from 1956 until his assassination in September 1959, the Bandaranaike monument which weighs a hefty 5 tons (5,080kg) was a gift from the Russians. Set on its own little hillock, this is a good place to gaze at the ocean and watch the cars whiz by.

To the left of the open expanse of the **Galle Face Green** is the **Taj Samudra Hotel** and at the far end is the historically famous **Galle Face Hotel**, built in 1864. Further down Galle Road is **Hotel Lanka Oberoi**. The new wing has a basement art gallery with some fine paintings by Sri Lanka's best known artist, Senaka

The temple on Beira Lake

Senanayake. Beside the Oberoi is **Araliyagaha Madiraya** (Temple Trees), the official residence of the Prime Minister. Cars are not encouraged to stop here for security reasons, but strollers will be able to glimpse through the closed gates a large garden and a substantial white building.

Virtually opposite are the **American** and **British embassies**, both imposing in their different styles. The British flag pole is said to be slightly higher than the American one because the spy sent out to find out the exact height bungled it. When the true nature of his probing questions were uncovered, the British misled the American spy with the wrong measurement.

This is also **Kollupitiya**, the shopping area of Colombo's elite. A turn left from Galle Road to Dharmapala Mawatha at the traffic lights reveals the **market** and on the right the island's first shopping complex, **Liberty Plaza**.

The market sells fresh meat and a diverse array of fresh fish and seafood. The beautifully arranged displays of fruit and vegetables are grown in Sri Lanka and show the wide variety available. The shopkeepers may well offer a taste. Why not accept the invitation?

Moving along Dharmapala Mawatha, there is a wide range of brassware laid out on the pavement, just before the traffic lights where the road crosses Sir James Peiris Mawatha. Take a look but be warned that prices are not cheap. Turn left at the lights and after 200yds (180m), a very pretty sight can be seen on the left side – a **Buddhist temple** in the waters of the **Beira Lake**.

Stop and walk to the temple on the wooden platform. Inside are statues, some from Thailand, and antiques which the head monk has collected. Beside the temple is a *bo* tree (*Ficus religiosa*), representing the tree under which the Buddha gained enlightenment. The temple is part of the **Gangarama Temple**, and in February the streets take on a festive air when the Navam Perehera (procession) parades through the streets, attracting hundreds of thousands of spectators. Next to the famous Kandy Perehera, it is one of the biggest pageants in Sri Lanka today.

The neighbouring area is called **Slave Island** because slaves were kept here during the time of the Dutch. Crocodiles were used to guard them and to prevent any means of escape, no boats were allowed on the lake after dark. The Sinhala name is **Kompanna Vidiya** (Company Street) because a company of Malay soldiers were stationed here during the time of the British.

Go down Sir James Peiris Mawatha along the lake to Wekanda Road and turn right. This is fast becoming a bankers' road, with the National Development Bank, Sampath and Amro banks having their headquarters there. Turn left onto R A de Mel Mawatha and then left to Perehera Mawatha. The white wall around the lake here is modelled after the Kandyan hill country style.

At Sir James Peiris Mawatha, turn right and after 400ft (120m) turn left at Ramanayake Mawatha. Go right at the next junction, Hunupitiya Cross Road, park the car near the *Sunday Times* press and walk the 50yds (45m) to Dharmapala Mawatha and visit the arts and crafts shop, **Lakmedura**. Brassware, silverware, wood carvings, gems, jewellery, leather products, batiks and lace are all here.

Return to the car and turn left at Dharmapala Mawatha. On our right is **Viharamahadevi Park**, renamed from Victoria Park in honour of the mother of Sri Lanka's national hero, Dutugemunu.

Turn right at F R Senanayake Mawatha. At the entrance to the park on the right is a giant statue of the Buddha while on the side is one of Viharamahadevi. The park is beautifully maintained with flower beds and green turf amidst giant trees. On the left is the **Colombo Town Hall**. Turn left at the end of F R Senanayake Mawatha to Dr C W W Kannangara Mawatha. On the left is the white, 100-year-old **Devatagaha Mosque.** Beggars gather here in the evenings to seek alms. Turn round at Lipton's Circus, where the two giants of the tea industry, Lipton and Brooke Bond, have their offices. For lunch, try the set meal

Devatagaha Mosque

Lanka's 'Capitol Hill', the Colombo Town Hall

at **Don Stanley's**, a cozy restaurant on Kannangara Mawatha, costing Rs 350.

After lunch, drive beyond the roundabout, where C W W Kannangara Mawatha becomes Albert Crescent. On the right is an imposing white building, the **Colombo National Museum** (open daily 9am–5pm, closed on Friday, Tel: 694767) where there is a good collection of artifacts. You may wish to come back another day to spend a longer time here (See *Itinerary 3*). After the museum, turn left to Albert Crescent and right at the roundabout to Horton Place, near the petrol kiosk. In this residential area are some fine examples of Sri Lankan-style houses, both old and new. At 21 Horton Place lives Dr Gamani Corea, one of Sri Lanka's best known economists. His house is over 90 years old and though not open for public visits, you may peer over the gate and get a glimpse of a comfortable, well-ventilated house and verandah designed for gracious living in a tropical climate.

Continue straight pass two sets of traffic lights to Castle Street. Take the road to the island's new capital, **Sri Jayewardenepura Kotte**. Turn right at the sign to the **Parliament**. Even from a distance, the new Parliamentary Complex is a beautiful sight with its Kandyan architectural style poised in the middle of the Diyawanna Oya lake. Unfortunately, tight security prevents the public from getting close. Kotte was one of the ancient capitals of Lanka and the king was in residence here when the Portuguese arrived in 1505, the first Westerners to colonise the island.

Return towards Castle Street but at the roundabout in front of Tickell Road, turn left towards Bauddhaloka Mawatha. On the left is Model Farm Road leading to Colombo's 18-hole **Golf Course**, where visitors can play for a nominal fee.

Drive straight on past the Kanatta Cemetery and turn right at the roundabout along Bauddhaloka Mawatha. About half a mile (1km) on this road to the left is the **Bandaranaike Memorial International Conference Hall** (BMICH), the venue of the SAARC meeting in November 1991. The octagonal BMICH has an interesting history. A gift from the Chinese government to Sri Lanka in memory of Mr S W R D Bandaranaike and completed in 1975, it is a showpiece convention centre which can accommodate up to 1,500.

Why is it called the BMICH? There lies an interesting story. The proposed name was Bandaranaike International Conference Hall until Mrs Sirima Bandaranaike, his widow and then Prime Minister, was told that the acronym of the four words (BICH) may not be appropriate and that the word 'Memorial' should be added.

To the right of the BMICH is a replica of the **Aukana Buddha Statue**, the original being carved out of sheer rock around AD400. Further down Bauddhaloka Mawatha are the offices of the state-owned television and radio stations. Turn right on Maitland Place, the first road after the BMICH, then right into Independence Square which leads to the **Independence Commemoration Hall**, where the independence ceremony was held on February 4, 1948. The building, open on both sides, is modelled on a Kandyan-style royal audience pavilion.

For dinner, try the **Seafish Restaurant** (Tel: 326915) at 15 Sir Chittampalam Gardiner Mawatha, behind the Regal Cinema, about 400yds (365m) from the Renaissance Hotel.

3. The Colombo National Museum

Artifacts of ancient Lanka in a British colonial building, including the priceless gem-encrusted Sinhala throne. Half-day tour.

If there is no time to see the ancient cities of Sri Lanka (see *Excursion 13*), a visit to the **Colombo Museum** (open daily 9am–5pm, closed on Friday, admission fee: Rs 40, Tel: 694767) will provide a taste of the richness of the history and culture of the island. It is interesting to note that the first concept of a museum in the world was recorded in 307–267BC in the 19th chapter of the *Mahavamsa*, the monks' chronicle of the island's history.

Drive down Galle Road from Colombo Fort to the Kollupitiya Junction. Turn left to Dharmapala Mawatha and go down to Viharamahadevi Park. Turn right at the roundabout. Half a mile (1km) along Albert Crescent, the museum can be seen on the left. Built in 1887 by British Governor Sir William Gregory, the imposing white building is an example of architecture introduced by the British. There are two bookshops at the entrance selling postcards at Rs 1.50, the cheapest on the island.

The limestone Buddha statue (AD300–500) at the museum entrance, originally found at Toluvila, near Anuradhapura, will catch your attention. Near the staircase are two 12th-century carvings

Colombo Museum, a treasure trove of artifacts

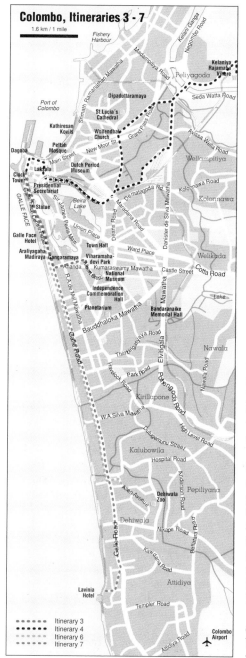

Colombo, Itineraries 3 - 7

1.6 km / 1 mile

Fishery Harbour
Madampitiya Mawatha
Keliani Ganga
Negombo Road
Kelaniya Rajamaha Vihare
Peliyagoda
Shrimath Ramanathan Mawatha
Dipaduttaramaya
Seda Watta Road
Port of Colombo
St. Lucia's Cathedral
Kathiresan Kovils
Wolfendhal Church
New Moor St.
Grand Pass Road
Avissa Wella Road
Wellampitiya
Peltah Mosque
Main Street
Dutch Period Museum
Dagoba
Clock Tower
Lakgala
Presidential Secretariat
Beira Lake
Dematagoda Rd
Maradena Road
Kolonnawa Road
Kolonnawa
Statue
Sir James Peiris Mw
Deans Road
Daniste de Silva Mawatha
Galle Face Hotel
Union Place
Araliyagaha Madiraya
Town Hall
Ward Place
Welikada
Gangaramaya
Viharamaha-devi Park
Ananda
Kumaraswamy Mawatha
Castle Street
Cotta Road
National Museum
Mawatha
R.A.de Mel Mawatha
Independence Commemoration Hall
Lake
Planetarium
Baddhaloka Mawatha
Bandaranaike Memorial Hall
Nawala
Galle Road
Thimongesula Road
Elvitigala
Nawala Road
Harelock Road
Park Road
Pohengoda Road
Kirillapone
W.A.Silva Mawatha
Dulugemunu Street
High Level Road
Kalubowila
Hospital Road
Anderson Road
Allen Avenue
Dehiwala Zoo
Pepiliyana
Galle Road
Dehiwala
Nikape Road
Bellanta Road
Kaw dara Road
Attidiya
Lavinia Hotel
Templer Road
Attidiya Road
Colombo Airport

•••••• Itinerary 3
▪▪▪▪▪▪ Itinerary 4
•••••• Itinerary 6
•••••• Itinerary 7

taken from a rock carving of seven goddesses found in Polonnaruwa, and a carving of the 10th-century Hindu goddess Durga found at Anuradhapura. Though not marked, this is **Gallery 1**. One of the three guides available to visitors can take you around. Tip the guide at your own discretion.

In **Gallery 2** are clothes worn by nobles. Watch out for horn combs used by the aristocracy. This gallery also contains a fine example of a moonstone and guard stones. There are no protective railings, and details of the intricate rock carvings can be clearly seen.

In **Gallery 4** are bronze statues, lamps, carvings of Hindu goddesses, and pottery of the 3rd and 4th century. Also on display are some fine examples of 12th-century Chinese bowls found during excavations at Polonnaruwa.

In **Gallery 6**, look out especially for the bronze brassware which depict the cruel deaths of Ehelepola Kumarihamy's children, ordered by the last king of Sri Lanka. There are also some fine examples of wood and ivory carvings of the 17th and 19th century.

A visit to **Gallery 8** is a must for the ancient swords and guns of Sri Lankan kings. Note the old Sinhala gun with intricate carvings on the brass plates, and the sword used by King Buvenekabahu of

Yapahuwa. The prize exhibit, of course, is the gem-studded throne of Sri Lankan kings, originally built for King Rajasinghe I (1636–87). Even his footstool is studded with gems. Just beside the throne sits an equally ostentatious bejewelled crown.

The museum's paintings, dating back centuries, tell a tale of a bygone era when the pace was more relaxed. There are scenes of Sri Lanka's aborigines, the Veddahs, hunting with bows and arrows. Look out for the *olas* (palm-leaves) on which Buddhist monks patiently recorded the island's history.

For researchers, the **Museum Library** has over half a million publications of interest. For children, the fascinating world of puppetry comes alive with the display upstairs. There are masks used in traditional dance, including devil dancing.

The **National Museum of Natural History** (open daily 9am–5pm, admission fee: Rs 25), behind the main museum, has many fine examples of Sri Lanka's wildlife and other natural resources.

4. Kelaniya Rajamaha Vihare

A half-day tour to the Kelaniya Temple. See the chair on which the Buddha reputedly sat when he preached for peace.

Festival celebration at Kelaniya

Drive west from Colombo Fort and turn right after crossing the Kelaniya Bridge. Then turn right soon after Peliyagoda to the road which leads to the **Kelaniya Rajamaha Vihare** temple, a distance of about 7 miles (11km).

This *dagoba* is unusual. It is not round like those found in most parts of the island, but shaped like a heap of paddy. The history of the temple dates back to over 2,500 years. It is believed the Buddha visited here and preached from a jewelled chair to warring factions on the futility of fighting. The original *dagoba* was said to have enshrined the chair but was later destroyed by South Indian invaders. Restored in the 13th century, the Kelaniya Temple again suffered at the hands of invaders in the 16th century, this time the Portuguese.

The reclining Buddha and the Buddha in meditative pose are two important statues here, but it is possible to spend hours just looking at the extraordinary frescoes depicting the life of the Buddha and important events in the island's history.

There is the story of King Kelanitissa who boiled a Buddhist monk alive in oil because he suspected him of trying to pass a love letter to the Queen. The angry gods raised tidal waves and the King was told that the only way to appease the gods was to sacrifice his

30

daughter to the sea. The King obeyed the wishes of the wise ones; the seas calmed and the daughter who was swept out to sea on a boat landed at Kirinda. King Kavantissa of the south married her and she became the mother of perhaps the best known of the island's kings, Dutugemunu.

The temple is a hive of activity on the full moon of January, when hundreds of elephants and thousands of dancers parade the streets during the Duruthu Perehera festival.

5. Galle Face Green

Politics, vendors and kite fliers in the centre of Colombo. Spend a few hours watching the many faces of Colombo here.

Drive south on the main artery road from Colombo Fort past the Presidential Secretariat to **Galle Face Green**. This largest open space in Colombo could tell many a tale. It is many things to people: an ideal spot for lovers who hide from gazing crowds and the sun behind umbrellas; a playground for children with roadside vendors selling brightly-coloured balloons, kites, toys, soft drinks and ices; an arena for professionals to debate issues of the day; and a popular hangout for teenagers.

Observe local colour like the kite seller who displays hundreds of fluttering discs of myriad colours. In the evening, vendors push their carts laden with banana chips and fried lentils to vantage points.

Galle Face Hotel

Whether rich or poor, Galle Face has no barriers. The Green has seen political rallies and musical extravaganzas. It was used for horse racing a century ago and the promenade along the sea, stretching for nearly a mile, was built in 1859 by the British Governor Sir Henry Ward for 'the ladies and children of Colombo'. Thanks to his foresight, the Green retains much of its old charm, with no buildings to mar the beauty of the wide open space.

On one side is **Galle Face Hotel**. Boasting yesterday's charms and today's luxury, it is the oldest hotel this side of the Suez. Due to its eccentric chairman, the hotel retains much of the old style without much care for comfort or service. A wing remains closed at a time tourists are crying out for nostalgia. Note the hotel's hand-carved doors, manned by the doorman in traditional dress. The hotel has some fine old furniture and the ballroom – now used mainly for weddings – boasts of high ceilings, balconies and memories of a bygone era. With a cool beer or long drink in hand, sit on the verandah and watch the sunset.

Halfway down across the road is the statue of a former Prime Minister of Sri Lanka, S W R D Bandaranaike, who paid the supreme sacrifice for trusting people too much. He was slain after only three years in office.

6. The Dehiwala Zoo

Both adults and youngsters will enjoy a few hours at this zoo. Cap the day by watching a performance of dancing elephants.

The **Dehiwala Zoo** (open daily 8.30am–6pm, Tel: 712751) is one of the finest in Asia and its sprawling acres are host to a variety of animals and birds. Drive 6 miles (9km) from Colombo, south along the Galle Road. Turn left at Allen Avenue, Dehiwala, and follow the signposts.

It is pleasing to see many animals in their natural habitat. Whether it be lions, bears, tigers, rhinos, giraffes or gorillas, there is a greater freedom here than in many zoos around the world. The sight of painted storks fishing in the pond or screeching macaws ruffling their bright feathers immediately puts any visitor at ease.

In the **Reptile House** you will find a rare albino cobra and an enormous python. Watch out for the little tortoises which take piggy-back rides on the backs of ferocious crocodiles. The zoo also has an excellent collection of primates.

Do not miss the 500 varieties of marine life at the **Mini Medura** (aquarium), constructed with children in mind who dart around the exhibit like the fish in the tanks. The **Nocturnal House** allows visitors to see creatures like owls and lemurs in their natural habitat.

The highlight of the zoo is the elephant circus which comes on daily at 5.15pm, with extra shows on Sunday and holidays at 3.15pm. The huge pachyderms perform all sorts of antics like standing on their heads, wiggling their backs to music, hopping on one foot and standing up on their hind legs.

When the biggest of the elephants begins to play a soundless mouth organ, the other elephants start skipping and trooping behind. There is an exciting moment when an elephant places a foot on the ma-

Too big for his seat

hout's stomach and lifts him by the head using its mouth. The end of the performance signals a mass exodus from the zoo. It's best to get your bearings to the exit so that you can quickly make your way out and catch a taxi back to Colombo.

7. Mount Lavinia

Yearning for a sandy beach and the crash of waves but too lazy to drive too far out? Head for Mount Lavinia, only 8 miles (13km) from Colombo.

To the sailors of the 19th century, **Mount Lavinia** stood out like the silhouette of a pregnant wench along the southern coastline. This is one of the loveliest beach areas close to any metropolis in the world, being a mere 8 miles (13km) from the heart of the city of Colombo.

To get there, drive south along Galle Road from Colombo Fort and turn right to Hotel Road half a mile (1.6km) past the Mount Lavinia cemetery. The focal point of Mount Lavinia is the **Mount Lavinia Hotel**, though there are others like the Mount Royal Beach Hotel which was built in the 1970s.

Mount Lavinia Hotel

Mount Lavinia Hotel was built in 1810 as a private residence by a fun-loving British Governor who constructed secret passages in the building. Some of these have been discovered in the kitchens, but unfortunately, are not open to the public.

Apparently, a *rodiya* (outcaste) girl who worked for the Governor fell in love with him. When the Governor was leaving, he asked the *rodiya* what she wanted from him. Much to his surprise, she did not ask for the house which he was willing to give her. Instead, she asked for official permission to wear a cloth about the waist, a mark of status normally denied to *rodiyas*. The Governor gave his consent with an official gazette notification and the house was sold and turned into a hotel.

On the beach there are little bathing huts which can be hired for the day. Lie in the sun and relax, take a dip when it gets too hot and enjoy the sights and sounds. There are pineapple and coconut vendors who sell drinks to quench your thirst, while others sell beads and shells.

There are signboards warning swimmers of strong undercurrents, so don't venture into deep waters. There is a good beach restaurant at the hotel, **La Langousterie**, open from 10am till 10.30pm.

Shopping

Gems, batiks and handicrafts are among the best buys in Sri Lanka. With the liberalisation of controls, a wide variety of imported goods are also available. Though the latter may not be as low as Hong Kong prices, the number of Indians who come to Colombo for shopping indicates that prices are cheaper than India. The main shopping areas are in the **Fort** and **Pettah**, though gem shops are ubiquitous throughout Colombo, including along **Galle Road** and **R A de Mel Mawatha**.

With the establishment of shopping complexes in Colombo, notably the **Liberty Plaza** in Kollupitiya and **Majestic City** in Bambalapitiya, there are now shopping hubs where a wide variety of well displayed and attractive items are available.

Gems

The variety of gems found on the island is immense and it is difficult to give prices as a guide as each stone is unique and its cost depends on factors such as colour, size and shape.

Blue sapphires are the best buy in Sri Lanka. Since the stones are not price-marked, bargaining is expected. Unless something really takes your fancy and you feel you must have it, it is best to look around and compare prices before purchasing.

Star sapphires and star rubies produce a gleam with six rays when light falls on them and are beautiful when set as rings and pendants. Alexandrites are olive green in natural light turning into raspberry red under artificial light.

Cat's Eye, so-called because it has a streak of light in the middle, as in the eye of a cat, comes in hues of honey yellow or apple green. Other popular stones are amethysts, garnets, aquamarines, topaz and moonstones.

Recommended jewellery stores include **Premadasa & Co** at Sir Baron Jayatilleke

An array of sparkling stones

Lacquerware, masks and clay toys

Mawatha, Colombo 1, Tel: 548723; **Hemachandra Brothers**, 229 Galle Road, Colombo 4, Tel: 325147; and **Zam Gems** of 81 Galle Road, Colombo 4, Tel: 580164. The government maintains its own gem dealership, the **State Gem Corporation**. You can approach this agency to verify the authenticity of any gem you have purchased.

Batiks

Batiks come in attractive colours and patterns and are often made into shirts, sarongs, saris, table cloths, wall hangings or even curtains. The most popular designs are motifs of elephants, peacocks and Kandyan dancers. **Barefoot** at Hotel Ceylon Intercontinental and **Vipula's** at Renaissance Hotel stock a good variety.

Ceramics

Noritake ceramics at bargain prices are one of the attractions in Sri Lanka. The sets are made in Sri Lanka and both export quality and factory seconds with small flaws are available in a wide variety of colours and designs at **Ceylon Ceramics Corporation** (open Monday–Saturday 10am–5.45pm), 696 Galle Road, Colombo 3.

Handicrafts

Mats, masks, drums, coconut shell dolls, boxes made from porcupine quills, lace, reed, basket and bambooware, lacquerware,

wooden figurines, shell crafts, silver and brassware are the most popular handicraft items. Elephants, painted batik style or carved from ebony wood, also make nice souvenirs to bring home.

Shops recommended are **Laksala**, York Street, Colombo 1; **Lakmedura**, 113 Dharmapala Mawatha, Colombo 7, Tel: 328900; and **Lakpahana**, 21 Race Course Avenue, Colombo 7, Tel: 692554. All shops are open 9am–5.30pm from Monday to Saturday.

Cashew Nuts

This is the fruit Sri Lankans call 'the one which caught God napping'. The story goes that as this was the last fruit

Don't leave Sri Lanka without a packet or two of tea

to be created, there was no time to insert the seed before the stroke of midnight. This is why the cashew seed hangs under the fruit, not inside it. Cashews are available in packets, plain or roasted and are a delightful snack. For gifts, cashews packed in eye-catching containers can be bought at **Expo Shoppe** at Liberty Plaza Shopping Complex, Colombo 3.

Tea

Tea is synonymous with Sri Lanka. Even people who have never heard of Sri Lanka are familiar with Ceylon tea. It is the mainstay of the economy and the island is the world's largest exporter of high-quality Ceylon tea.

Being a hydroscopic product which absorbs moisture very quickly, tea must be carefully stored. Keep it in a cool, dry place and in a bottle with the lid tightly screwed on. When the bottle is opened, the cap must be replaced at the earliest possible moment. If these few rules are observed, the tea will keep well and provide you with countless cups. Tea for all palates is available, but the best brand is Broken Orange Pekoe (BOP). For gift items try the **Mlesna Tea Centre** which has branches at the Hilton, Liberty Plaza and Majestic City, Tel: 574545, and the **Senok Trade Combine** on R A de Mel Mawatha, Colombo 4, Tel: 580017.

Spices

Spices constitute the heart of the Sri Lanka's cuisine and an aromatic range from cumin to coriander is available packed in plain plastic packets or in beautiful boxes. Try **The Spice Shop** on the first floor of Unity Plaza in Colombo 4 at the Bambalapitiya Junction, Tel: 501622.

Leather Products

Fine quality leather crafted into belts, shoes, handbags, leather jackets, wallets, purses and skirts are some of the products available. Leather items are often sold by pavement vendors. Made to order shoes cost about Rs 2,000, but prices often depend on design, size and how soon you want them delivered.

Antiques

A number of antique shops in Colombo stock art objects including old gramophones, clocks and Buddhist statues. But the best shops are found near Mount Lavinia, 8 miles (13km) from Colombo. **Raux Brothers**, 164 Galle Road, Dehiwala, Tel: 713457 and **Treasure Trove** at 247 Galle Road, Mount Lavinia, Tel: 717253 are recommended. **Buhary & Co** have a shop with a nice selection of antiques at the Colombo Marriot Hotel (Tel: 541149). Remember that objects over 50 years old cannot be exported.

Aladdin's treasure trove

Eating Out

If variety is the spice of life, then the spices of Sri Lanka will surely titillate the palate. There are different spices for different curries – tried, tested and handed down for generations. One also has to consider the island's heritage of dishes handed down by its traders and conquerors. Very much part of Sri Lankan cuisine are some old Dutch and Portuguese foods like *bolo fiado* (laminated cake) and *boroa* (semolina biscuits). *Biryani*, a traditional Muslim rice and meat dish and Tamil *thosai* (pancakes) and *vade* (fritters), have become indigenous to Sri Lankan cuisine.

Rice is the staple and there are over 15 varieties in Sri Lanka. I personally prefer the red country rice, *Kakuluhaal*. This strain of rice is full of vitamins and has a unique nutty

The art of making fine hoppers

flavour as the grains are left unpolished. White rice, whether it be the ball-shaped *Sambha*, the long-grained *Basmati* or the white *Milchard*, are widely available.

If you want to go native and eat your food with your fingers, the waiter will always oblige with a finger bowl.

Rice is used in a variety of dishes. In the morning, it can be used for *Kiribath* (milk rice), made with rice cooked in coconut milk or fresh milk and spices. This is considered an auspicious meal and is normally eaten at special occasions – on the first of each month, or to welcome visitors.

Indiappa (string hoppers) is the Sri Lankan version of a combination of Italian spaghetti and Chinese noodles. A batter of rice or white flour mixed with water is squeezed through a special perforated instrument onto bamboo or woven plastic trays and then steam-cooked till fluffy.

String hopper *biryani* – a lunch or dinner delicacy – is produced by breaking an *indiappa* into small pieces and then cooking them with spices, meat and cashews. *Appa* (hoppers), made of rice or white flour added to coconut milk and yeast and made into a pancake with crispy edges is a favourite Sri Lankan breakfast preparation. *Lamprais* is a Dutch variation. Rice and curries are cooked and then wrapped in a banana leaf and steamed with chicken or beef. Costing about Rs 50 each, it is available in most pastry shops in Colombo. *Pittu* is ground rice or white flour mixed with coconut and then steam-cooked in a special container made of bamboo. *Pittu* is eaten with coconut milk, sometimes with meat or fish.

Among the Muslims, the *godamba roti* is an interesting dish. It is fascinating to see this being made, where with each turn of the wrist of an expert handler, a small ball of flour becomes longer and flatter. Another favourite is *watallappan*, made of *jaggery*, eggs, milk and cashew nuts – a delicious but rich and heavy dessert.

Locally made brews are popular. Beer usually comes in large bottles. The beer made with water from the hills of Nuwara Eliya by Ceylon Breweries is an invigorating drink. To get a taste of a real Sri Lankan product, try *arrack*. Made from coconut and distilled in large vats, it's the cheapest form of alcohol and is widely available. Toddy, made from the coconut or *kitul* tree, is also popular.

For teetotallers, there are plenty of fruit juices, though the most popular are passion fruit and lime juice. Imported beer, drinks and juices are expensive because there is a whopping 100 percent tax on these items.

A three-course meal for two people without drinks is categorized as follows: Expensive = Rs 750 and above; Moderate = Rs500–Rs750; Inexpensive = less than Rs 500.

Buffet under the stars

Fresh corn in Trincomalee

Restaurants in Colombo

Sri Lankan

BANANA LEAF RESTAURANT
86 Galle Road, Colombo 4
Tel: 584403
Go native and eat off a banana leaf. Known for their ambrosial crab dishes. Inexpensive.

HOTEL DE BUHARI
15 Panchikawatte Road, Colombo 10
Tel: 431015
A fine selection of Sri Lankan dishes. For local flavour, try the Basmati rice *biryani* on weekends. Inexpensive.

CURRY BOWL
24 Deal Place, Colombo 3
Tel: 575157
A good introduction to the spicy hot curries of Sri Lanka. Inexpensive.

IBN BATUTA
Renaissance Hotel
Tel: 544200
For something sweet, try the *watal-lappan* for dessert. Moderate.

RANMALU
Hotel Lanka Oberoi
Tel: 321001
Good selection of Sri Lankan and Indian food at this Oberoi outlet. Moderate.

HOTEL RENUKA
Galle Road, Colombo 3
Tel: 573598, 573602
Sri Lankan cuisine complemented by the food of Jaffna. Inexpensive.

Chinese

CHINESE DRAGON CAFE
232 Galle Road, Colombo 4
Tel: 588144, 502733
The cheapest place for Chinese food, but service is slow. Inexpensive.

CHINESE PARK VIEW LODGE
70 Park Street, Colombo 2
Tel: 326255
Wide range of Chinese dishes. Try the *kankun* with beef. Inexpensive.

EASTERN PALACE
253 R A de Mel Mawatha, Colombo 3
Tel: 573436
Famous for its shell lagoon prawns. Moderate.

FLOWER DRUM RESTAURANT
26 Thurstan Road, Colombo 3
Tel: 574216, 574811
Try the hot plate sizzlers and the lemon chicken. Moderate.

LONG FENG
Renaissance Hotel
Tel: 544200
If you've never tried cuttlefish before, this is the place. Wonderful stir-fried with mushrooms. Expensive.

Indian

NAVRATNA
Hotel Taj Samudra
Tel: 446622
Excellent North Indian cuisine and cosy ambience. Expensive.

SARAS
25 Charles Drive, Colombo 3

Tel: 575226
A taste of two cultures. Indian and Chinese food in this renowned restaurant. Closed on Monday. Moderate.

SHANTHI VIHAR
3 Havelock Road, Colombo 5
Tel: 580224
The *chana bhathura* is an excellent preparation. Inexpensive.

Japanese

GINZA HOSHEN
Colombo Hilton Hotel
Tel: 544644
Try the *shabu shabu* here. Expensive.

JAPANESE DOLL
32B Sir Mohammed Macan Markar Mawatha, Colombo 3
Tel: 446589
Charming decor complements the authentic Japanese cuisine. Moderate.

KARAOKE RESTAURANT
Renaissance Hotel
Tel: 544200
New floating restaurant. The *tepanyaki* is a favourite. Moderate.

Korean

ARI RANG
16 Abdul Cafoor Mawatha, Colombo 3
Tel: 575186
Serves both Korean and Chinese cuisine under the same roof. Moderate.

HAN GOOK GWAN
62 Havelock Road, Colombo 5
Tel: 587961, 588109
A new restaurant. Try the steamboat. Moderate.

KOLIO
Hotel Empress, Colombo 3
Tel: 574930/1
A favourite among the Korean com-munity of Sri Lanka – an endorsement that speaks volumes. Moderate.

Pakistani

KEBABISH
526 Galle Road, Colombo 3
Tel: 574479
The only place to get genuine Pakistani food. Kebabs are juicy and full of flavour. Moderate.

Seafood

SEA FISH
15 Sir Chittampalam Gardiner Mawatha, Colombo 2
Tel: 326915
A speciality seafood restaurant serving almost everything that swims. Moderate.

Selling snacks at the seafront

Continental

DON STANLEY'S
59 Alexander Place, Colombo 7
Tel: 686486
Family-owned restaurant run by a former beauty queen. Moderate.

GABLES
Colombo Hilton Hotel
Tel: 544644
Excellent atmosphere, but small portions. Free copy of *International Herald Tribune* with lunch. Expensive.

German Restaurant
11 Galle Face Court, Colombo 3
Tel: 421577
Cosy German atmosphere, and friendly staff. Moderate.

London Grill
Hotel Lanka Oberoi
Tel: 320001
Popular English-style steakhouse. Moderate.

Noblesse
Renaissance Hotel
Tel: 544200
For fine Continental cuisine and wines. Moderate.

Palms Supper Club
Hotel Ceylon Intercontinental
Tel: 421221
Excellent Continental cuisine matched by beautiful views. Expensive.

Supper Club
Hotel Lanka Oberoi
Tel: 320001
Excellent view and entertainment. Try the specials. Expensive.

Italian

Il Ponte Ristorànte
Colombo Hilton Hotel
Tel: 544644
Authentic Italian cuisine; try the excellent ravioli. Moderate.

Pizzeria
Hotel Ceylon Intercontinental
Tel: 421221
The cheapest pizzas are at this open-air restaurant. Good value for money. Moderate.

Swiss

Chesa Swiss
3 Deal Place A, Colombo 3
Tel: 573433
Cheese fondue is full of flavour. Closed on Sundays. Expensive.

Hotel Coffee Shops
(open 24 hours a day)

Emerald
Hotel Ceylon Intercontinental
Tel: 421221
Overlooking the sea, a popular place for lunch. Moderate.

Gardenia
Holiday Inn
Tel: 422001
Excellent Moghul food. Moderate.

Le Brasserie
Hotel Marriot
Tel: 544544
Popular for hamburgers and pizza. Nice atmosphere. Moderate.

Lotus Terrace
Colombo Hilton Hotel
Tel: 544644
Lovely setting. Try the Sri Lankan speciality – *lamprais* cooked in banana leaf. Moderate.

Ports of Call
Hotel Taj Samudra
Tel: 446622
Try the piquant and Portuguese-inspired dishes from Goa, South India. Moderate.

Purple Orchid
Hotel Lanka Oberoi
Tel: 421171, 320001
A good outlet for quick meals. Overlooks a lovely garden. Moderate.

Summerfields
Renaissance Hotel
Tel: 544200
The best lunch-time buffet in town. Moderate.

EXCURSIONS

8. Kandy, the Hill Capital

Journey through pineapple country, a cashew village and the world's only elephant orphanage; climb the hills of Utuwankanda and Kadugannawa to the hill country of Kandy for spectacular views and cool breezes; visit the fascinating Temple of the Tooth. Stay overnight, or drive through the grounds of the Peradeniya University Campus before heading back to Colombo.

The road to Kandy is an exciting one, racing through lowlands then climbing steep passes into what was once the citadel of power of Sri Lankan kings in the early 19th century. The road you will be driving on, the AI, is in good condition and was the first built by the British. Depart about 6.30am, as there is much to see. If fresh pineapples are enough for breakfast, then have it while on the way.

Leave Colombo and turn right at the Kelani Bridge onto the Kandy Road. About 16 miles (26km) from Colombo, near **Yakkala**, rows of pineapple stalls line the roadside. The best and sweetest pineapples in the country are grown right here. Take a break to feast on the freshly plucked fruit. Prices can vary from Rs 5 to Rs 30, depending on the season.

Caneware at Wewaldeniya

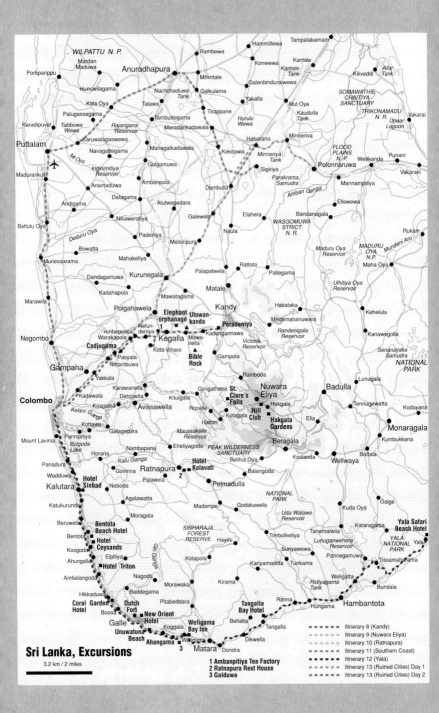

WILPATTU N.P.

Pomparippu
Mardan
Maduwa
Anuradhapura
Rambewa
Hammillewa
Tampalakamam
Konwewa
Kantale
Kantale
Tank
Kiliveddi
Allai
Tank
Hundwilagama
Mihintale
Galkulama
Galenbindunuwewa
SOMAWATHIE
CHAITIYA
SANCTUARY
Kala Oya
Nachchaduwa
Tank
Yakalla
Alut Oya
TRIKONAMADU
N.R.
Vakarai
Karadipuval
Palugassegama
Talawa
Tirappane
Hurulu
Wewa
Kaudulla
Tank
Upaar
Lagoon
Puttalam
Tabbowa
Wewa
Karuwalagaswewa
Rajangana
Reservoir
Tambuttegama
Maradankadawala
Habarana
Minneriva
FLOOD
PLAINS
N.P.
Welikanda
Punani
Madurankuli
Navagattegama
Mi Oya
Mahagalkadawala
Kekirawa
Minneriya
Tank
Sigiriya
Polonnaruwa
Vakaneri
Inginimitiya
Reservoir
Galgamuwa
Dambulla
Parakrama
Samudra
Mannampitiya
Andigama
Anamaduwa
Ambanpola
Elahera
Bandanagala
Ellewewa
Battulu Oya
Dalagama
Alutwegedara
Galewela
Naula
WASGOMUWA
STRICT
N.R.
Rukam
Deduru Oya
Nikaweratiya
Padeniya
Melsiripura
Maduru Oya
Reservoir
MADURU
OYA
N.P.
Mundeni Aru
Munessarama
Bowatta
Mahakeliya
Rattota
Pallegama
Maha Oya
Dandagamuwa
Kurunegala
Palapatwela
Ulhitiya Oya
Reservoir
Marawila
Kadahapola
Mawatagama
Matale
Hasalaka
Kehelula
Polgahawela
Kandy
Medamahanuwara
Kanawegolla
Negombo
Ambepussa
Warakapola
Nelun-
deniya
Elephant
orphanage
Utuwan-
kanda
Peradeniya
Kadungannawa
Randenigala
Reservoir
Senanayake
Samudra
NATIONAL
PARK
Cadjugama
Kegalla
Mawa-
nella
Kota Vihare
Victoria
Reservoir
Lunugala
Gampaha
Pasyala
Nittambuwa
Bible
Rock
Gampola
Badulla
Yakkala
Kadawata
Karawanella
Ginigathena
St.
Clare's
Falls
Ramboda
Nuwara
Eliya
Hakgala
Tennugewatta
Kodayana
Colombo
Kosgama
Dehiowita
Avissawella
Kitulgala
Rozelle
Kotagala
Hill
Club
Ella
Kelani Ganga
Kottawa
Hatton
Hakgala
Gardens
Monaragala
Mount Lavinia
Pannipitiya
Bolgoda
Lake
Galagedara
Maussakelle
Reservoir
PEAK WILDERNESS
SANCTUARY
Beragala
Kumbukkana
Horana
Nambapana
Eheliyagoda
Belihul Oya
Koslanda
Buttala
Panadura
Kalu Ganga
Govinna
Ratnapura
Hotel
Kalavati
Balangoda
Wellwaya
Wadduwa
Hotel
Sinbad
Neboda
Palawela
Pelmadulla
NATIONAL
PARK
Galge
Kalutara
Agalawatta
Madampe
Godakawela
Uda Walawe
Reservoir
Kuda Oya
Katukurunda
Moragala
Timbolketiya
Tanamalwila
Kataragama
Yala Safari
Beach Hotel
Beruwela
Bentota
Beach Hotel
SINHARAJA
FOREST
RESERVE
Hayes
Lunuganwehera
Reservoir
YALA
NATIONAL
PARK
Yala
Bentota
Hotel
Ceysands
Kosgoda
Elpitiya
Kotapola
Suriyawewa
Pannegamuwa
Tissamaharama
Ahungalla
Hotel Triton
Nagoda
Morawaka
Kariyamaditta
Tunkama
Weligatta
Ambalangoda
Baddegama
Kirama
Ridiyagama
Tank
Bundala
Hikkaduwa
Coral Garden
Hotel
Boosa
Dutch
Fort
Pitabeddara
New Orient
Hotel
Tangalla
Bay Hotel
Ranna
Hungama
Hambantota
Galle
Koggala
Weligama
Bay Inn
Beliatta
Tangalla
Unuwatuna
Beach
Ahangama
Weligama
Dikwella
Matara
Dondra

Sri Lanka, Excursions

3.2 km / 2 miles

1 Ambanpitiya Tea Factory
2 Ratnapura Rest House
3 Galduwa

Itinerary 8 (Kandy)
Itinerary 9 (Nuwara Eliya)
Itinerary 10 (Ratnapura)
Itinerary 11 (Southern Coast)
Itinerary 12 (Yala)
Itinerary 13 (Ruined Cities) Day 1
Itinerary 13 (Ruined Cities) Day 2

The pleasant smell of roasted cashew nuts will invade your nostrils near the 29th mile post (47km) at **Cadjugama** (Village of Cashews), where women sell roasted cashews to passing motorists from roadside stalls. What first began as an attempt by bus drivers' wives to supplement their income soon developed into a village tradition. Near the 30th mile post (48km) is **Wewaldeniya** (Grove of Cane), where cane chairs and cane-crafted elephants, bamboo lamps and bamboo baskets can be bought from the roadside.

If there is time, make an optional side trip to **Kota Vihare**, an archaelogical site and birthplace of one of Sri Lanka's greatest kings, Parakramabahu the Great (1153–1186). To get there, turn right off the main road at Nelundeniya junction and get there via Dedigama. One of the most fascinating objects on view at the nearby **Archaeological Museum** (open 9am–4pm daily except Tuesday) is a brass elephant lamp, found within the *dagoba*. The lamp has an oil tray in which a brass elephant hangs from intricately-carved chains. When the wicks are lit and the oil falls below a certain level, the elephant exudes more oil. The design is based on a hydraulic principle, but one can only be amazed at the technology as the lamp was made over 800 years ago.

Return to the main road. Soon after the 45th mile post (72km) is the **Ambanpitiya Tea Factory**. The management welcomes visitors and a 20-minute tour demonstrates how tea is prepared, from the fresh green leaves arriving from the estates to the fermentation, crushing, and drying stages. It is then ready to be packed for the tea auctions in Colombo. Packets are available for sale and a cup of freshly-brewed tea and snacks can be had at very reasonable prices.

After a satisfying cuppa, race on to Karandupona; past Kegalle, a signboard marks the turn left to the **Pinnawela Elephant Orphanage**. Be warned: it is very easy to miss this turn if driving from Kandy to Colombo as there is no sign facing that road. The state-run orphanage is about a 3-mile (5-km) drive past small privately-run elephant sideshows. Don't stop but go for the real thing.

There are 48 elephants in the orphanage of various ages, from only a few weeks old to the fully mature. This is the only elephant orphanage in the world where abandoned wild baby elephants are cared for, having been lost by their herd or fallen into pits. These elephants are trained to work, and will eventually be given to temples or sold or exchanged for other animals with foreign zoos. The orphanage was highlighted in the news recently when they were able to successfully breed elephants in captivity.

It is best to visit the orphanage during feeding or bathing times. The very young are fed from bottles, very much like human babies. Feeding times are at 9.15am, 1.15pm and 5pm while

Cavorting elephants

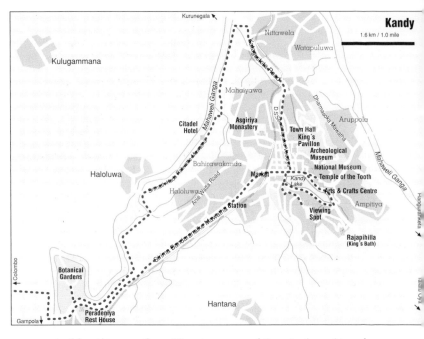

bathing times are from 10am to noon and 2pm to 4pm. At a given command, the older elephants guide the younger ones towards the river. They playfully squirt water on themselves and each other, and then lie down, hind legs first, immersing themselves completely except for their trunks. The mahouts climb on top of the larger elephants and help scrub them down. What better souvenir to remind you of this special place than a picture of a man taking a nap on

the back of a bathing elephant? There is a shop selling soft drinks and beer overlooking the elephant bath. Perch yourself on the riverside rocks and enjoy the entertaining scene.

Ceylon Hotels Corporation has a restaurant where drinks and lunch are available. A little spice garden in front of the entrance is run by the family who live there. The trees are not labelled so a tour without a guide is not of much value.

Return to the main road and turn left to resume the journey to Kandy. A lonely hill, **Utuwankanda**, signifies the place where Sri Lanka's Robin Hood, Saradiel, lived in the last century terrorising the rich to give to the poor. Unlike Robin Hood,

he had no greater cause and was finally captured and sentenced to death by the British.

The **Kadugannawa** climb starts near the 59th mile post (95km) and a sign appropriately announces a 'Thirst Aid Station'. A rubber hose pipe connected to a natural hillspring is conveniently placed for vehicles desperately in need of a fill-up of radiator water before the climb. The scenery from here is breathtaking, with terraced paddy fields, sheer drops and lush green vegetation. **Bible Rock** comes into view on the right, so named because it resembles an open bible.

Fruit stalls selling avocado and *durian* (a pungent thorny fruit) are a common sight on your way from Kadugannawa to **Peradeniya**. Cross the Peradeniya Bridge and go towards Kandy and the **Citadel Hotel**, turning left to Srimath Kuda Ratwatte Mawatha, off the Peradeniya-Kandy road, about half a mile after Peradeniya town. After 3 miles (5km), the lovely hotel comes into view. Enjoy the buffet lunch at about 12.30pm, overlooking the swimming pool and fast-flowing Mahaweli, the island's longest river.

About 1.30pm, turn left from the hotel and continue on the journey along the Mahaweli for about 3 miles (5km). This road emerges at Katugastota. Here, turn right and drive about 2 miles (3km) towards Kandy, 1,600ft (488m) above sea level.

Kandy is perhaps the prettiest of all of Sri Lanka's cities, nestled among green hills with the lake as its centrepiece. This was the seat of the last king of Sri Lanka till the British captured him in 1815. Drive first along the lake on Lake Drive and go up **Rajapihilla Mawatha** to appreciate the full splendour of Kandy below. The Temple of the Tooth is on the right with a recently constructed golden roof. According to popular belief, the island in the middle is where the king kept his mistresses, or people who misbehaved. Mahouts of the two resident elephants here offer rides. It is best to negotiate the price before getting on as there is no fixed amount. Pay between Rs 25 and Rs 100, based on how long the ride is.

Return to Lake Drive and proceed towards the **Temple of**

Paddy field outside Kandy

The Temple of the Tooth

the Tooth, visible in the distance. The tooth of the Buddha which is enshrined in the octagonal temple was brought to Sri Lanka in the 4th century from India, hidden in the hair of a princess. It is one of the most venerated objects in the island. The relic has become not only Sri Lanka's most prized possession, but the very seal of sovereignty. A replica of the tooth is ceremonially paraded through the streets annually. This custom first began over 1,500 years ago, making it the oldest continuous historical pageant in the world. The procession, the **Esala Perehera**, is held in July–August during which hundreds of gaily-decked elephants and thousands of dancers parade the streets for 10 consecutive nights.

Get to the temple by about 2.15pm and obtain a permit to take photos. At the entrance is a stand to leave your shoes. In the surrounding moat, you will see hundreds of fish. Near the staircase are fine examples of carvings of elephants. If you are not lucky enough to be there during the Perehera celebrations, try and imagine an elephant climbing up the steps to receive the replica of the tooth. The tooth, secreted amidst seven *dagoba*-shaped caskets, is richly decorated with jewels and precious stones that have been presented over centuries by royalty. The tooth relic itself is not an open display, only the outermost casket of seven.

Temple of the Tooth carving

During Perehera, revel in the atmosphere of awe created by the bare-torsoed drummers beating a steady tattoo in white headdresses and sarongs, and the thousands of worshippers offering flowers. The tall wooden pillars are typical of Kandyan architecture. To the left is the museum where the remains of the magnificent tusker, Raja, can be seen. This elephant who carried the temple's treasure to Kandy was declared a national treasure before its death.

About 2.45pm (remember to get your shoes first) walk about 200ft (60m) to the statue of **Madduma Bandara**, the boy hero of 1814. The story goes that when the king of Kandy heard of a plot by one of his ministers to have him assassinated, he ordered the family to be killed. When Bandara's elder brother flinched from facing the executioner, the nine-year-old boy said, 'Fear not, dear brother. I will show you how to confront death'. With that, he walked boldly up to the executioner to meet his fate.

Drive on about ½ mile (1km) to the **Kandyan Arts and Crafts Association** showroom near the Red Cross. Founded in the early 1880s to protect and encourage genuine Kandyan arts and crafts, this association was the first enterprise of its kind in Sri Lanka. Here are fine examples of Dumbara hemp mats to be used as wall hangings, lacquerware and fine jewellery.

About 3.15pm, return to the Kandy-Peradeniya Road and stop at the **Royal Botanical Gardens**, once the pleasure gardens of the queen. Its 150 acres (61ha) is filled with tropical plants of every description. The entrance fee is Rs 50 per adult and an extra Rs 25 for the car. Turn right soon after entering the gardens to see the beautifully laid out flowers. The orchid house has some rare species while the plant house contains leafy house varieties. Other attractions are the giant banyan trees, the coco-de-mer (double coconut) from the Seychelles which sailors once thought grew in the sea, and the giant bamboo. There is a spice garden with labelled trees including cloves, cinnamon and nutmeg.

It's time to call it a day. Drive through the beautiful **Peradeniya University Campus** before taking the Kandy-Colombo road to the

Kandy Lake

capital. Leave by 4.30pm to reach the city about 7.30pm. Alternatively, you may wish to spend the night at the Citadel Hotel, or one of the Kandy hotels (prior reservation is necessary) to avoid the drive back.

If driving back, en route at **Warakapola**, near the 37th mile post (59km), stop at the sweetmeat stall of **Jinadasa Thalaguli**, to try a typical Sri Lankan sweet, *thalaguli (gingelly* or sesame balls). *Puhul dosi* (pumpkin toffee) is also a favourite. This Kandy trip can be extended to include the hill station of Nuwara Eliya (see *Itinerary 9*).

For those who love the hills and want to enjoy the salubrious climate, an extension of the Kandy visit to Nuwara Eliya is recommended. A full-day with the option of an overnight.

Nuwara Eliya still feels very British today, probably due to its setting and colonial-style houses. In 1818, a hunting party led by Dr John Davy, brother of scientist Sir Humphrey Davy, chanced upon Nuwara Eliya, four years after the Kandyan kingdom was ceded to the British. In 1828, the Governor, Sir Edward Barnes, turned the highland into a health resort and sanatorium for British officials wanting to escape the heat of the lowlands.

In 1847, Sir Samuel Baker, the explorer and discoverer of the source of the White Nile, decided to build a home there. Using elephant-drawn carts, Baker transported all that was necessary for an English country town, including a blacksmith's forge, Hereford cows and even a bailiff.

The Elizabethan-style mansion that was originally built for the Governor is today the Grand Hotel of Nuwara Eliya. Fashionable circles in Colombo like to converge there in April, when temperatures begin to rise in the commercial capital. The green hills, the cool weather, the beautiful lake and parks all combine to make it the most pleasant hill resort on the island.

To get there from Kandy, turn left past the Peradeniya Bridge towards Gampola. Follow the winding road and signposts to Nuwara Eliya. The air gets cooler and a cardigan will keep you warm on the drive up through verdant tea plantations and waterfalls. It is only 43 miles (69km) from Kandy but the drive can take nearly two hours because of the steep climb; longer if there is fog.

In Nuwara Eliya, drive through the town past the park on the left along Badulla Road for about ¼ mile (½km) and turn right on Grand Hotel Road. The 100-year-old, 114-room **Grand Hotel** (Tel: 052-2281) has a lovely lawn with brightly-coloured flower beds. If you have spent the

Ella: the entrance to the hill country from the south

The century-old Grand Hotel

day in Kandy and arrived late, the air will be nippy. Check into a large room with a fireplace and take a warm bath. If there's time, go for a stroll into town, a 5-minute walk from the hotel. If not, enjoy a drink at the bar and then go to the dining hall for dinner.

The next morning, after a buffet breakfast, drive out of the hotel, turn right and go about 6 miles (10km) on the Badulla Road to **Hakgala Gardens**.

Hakgala means the jaw rock, and popular belief is that the rocky mountain was brought here by Hanuman, the monkey god in the Hindu epic, *Ramayana*. Rama wanted Hanuman to go to the Himalaya and bring a medicinal plant which grew there. Hanuman reached the mountains but forgot the name. He did the next best thing, which was to bring a part of the Himalaya with him, hoping that the required plant would be included. A mile (1.6km) before the Hakgala Gardens on the right is another place associated with the *Ramayana*, the Sita temple where the kidnapped Sita, Rama's wife, was held captive.

The entrance fee to the garden is Rs 50 per passenger with another Rs 30 for the car. Drive through some beautifully laid out gardens and stop near the rose garden. About a 100 different varieties are planted here. There are exotic species, too, named after personalities ranging from Elizabeth Taylor to Theodore Roosevelt. Stroll through orchid houses, foliage houses and on to a lovely area with quaint bridges, rushing streams of water and what looks like every type of fern in the world. Most trees are labelled. A colony of monkeys live near the summer house and often perform antics for visitors, hoping to be fed. Return to

The Hakgala Gardens

Nuwara Eliya, past vegetable gardens on the hillsides and colourful stalls selling the produce by the road.

Visit the **Hill Club**, over a century old and a 2-minute walk behind the hotel. It was only in 1967 that Sri Lankans could join the Club as the British tea planters had previously guarded their domain jealously. But dwindling numbers did not help the Club's fortunes and membership was opened to the locals.

Nuwara Eliya Golf Club

Some of the members' complaints – recorded in a book kept in the hall – make fascinating reading. The one I like best is Mr P P Blackmore's made in September 1902: 'Would suggest use of Bromo toilet paper in the closets in place of the present stuff which is like cardboard'. The Club is very British in many ways, with hunting trophies of trout and deer displayed prominently. Some original encyclopedias line the library's shelves and its billiard table is a true antique.

About ¼ mile away (½ km) from the Hill Club along Grand Hotel Road is the 90-acre (36-ha) **Nuwara Eliya Golf Club**, established in 1889. The 18-hole golf course is one of the best in Asia and certainly one of the prettiest. It is said to be the only golf course where all the holes can either be seen from the Club House or followed by car.

For those interested in unexplained mysteries, the monument to the elephant hunter, Major Rogers, in the little cemetery behind the Club House, is worth looking at. He killed some 1,500 elephants over 10 years. He died, not trampled by an elephant but struck by lightning. Since then, the unfortunate man's grave has been struck twice by lightning.

Return to the Club entrance and follow the road to town via the Windsor Hotel to the daily fair. Here are colourful stalls of vendors selling everything from clothes, shoes, plastic goods and toys to vegetables and cooked food.

Walk past the souvenir shops in town to **Lake Gregory**, the lovely artificial lake which makes the town so pretty. The people lining the banks are not watching the dredging but are fortune hunters looking for gems.

Standing on the shores of the lake, you should see Mt Piduruta-lagala. **Pidurutalagala**, at the foot of which Nuwara Eliya rests, is the highest mountain in Sri Lanka at 8,281ft (2,524m). As Nuwara

Eliya is already 6,197ft (1,889m) high, climbing Pidurutalagala should not pose a problem. It takes only about 2 hours to walk up to the summit and from there, Nuwara Eliya below shines like a fairyland village. Unfortunately, it is not advisable to make the climb as soldiers who guard the state-owned television tower on the summit are under explicit orders to shoot all trespassers.

The **race course** on Badulla Road is only a shadow of its former glory but the strawberry and carnation plantation at the centre is interesting. Permission to see the plantation, however, must be obtained in Colombo.

Have a quick lunch at the hotel, check out and drive back to Colombo. En route, via Ginigathhena, look out on the right for **St Clare's Falls**, a spectacular view on any day. At **Kitulgala**, 60 miles (96km) from Colombo, just before reaching the town, is an inconspicuous sign which says 'Road to Bridge over River Kwai'. This was where David Lean's movie was filmed although the river and the bridge are found in Thailand. Leave the car and follow the footpath past quaint little village houses. Only the foundations remain by the rushing water, so close your eyes and imagine the rail across the bridge and Alec Guiness at his best.

Scenic St Clare's Falls

Turn left about 3 miles (5km) further to have refreshments at the 14-room **Kitulgala Resthouse** (Tel: 036-7528) with its lovely view of the Kelani River and countryside. On the walls are some photos taken during the filming of the movie. Continue the journey, turning right to Colombo or left to Ratnapura (see *Itinerary 10*) at Avissawella.

10. Ratnapura, the City of Gems

A day-long excursion to the City of Gems. Learn how gems are mined and cut and visit the Pothgul Vihare temple, built in the 1st century BC.

Ratnapura is only 63 miles (101km) from Colombo and is Sinbad's legendary valley of diamonds in the fairy tale *1001 Arabian Nights*, whose gems were used by Solomon to entice Sheba.

Travellers have long waxed eloquent about the island's rich treasures. Marco Polo speaks of the King of Lanka wearing a priceless ruby which was a span in length and without flaws. The island is renowned for stones of many hues.

If coming from Colombo, start early, no later than 7am, after a good breakfast. From the Colombo Fort area take the Galle Road

Tapping rubber

for about 4 miles (6km) to Dickmans Road, then turn left just before Saint Paul's Milagiriya Church. Turn right onto Havelock Road, which at Kirilapone becomes High Level Road. Travel on it towards Avissawella, 28 miles (45km) from Colombo, and take the right fork towards Ratnapura. If travelling from Nuwara Eliya, the journey is about 5 hours. Remember to turn left at Avissawella.

This is scenic **rubber** country and the road runs through endless plantations. Stop near a convenient tree to see containers, often empty coconut shells, collecting the milky white latex that drips down from the incision.

At **Eheliyagoda**, the gateway to gem land, new prosperity is evident in the shops and houses. Past the Kuruwita signpost, the **tea estates** begin. The two leaves and a bud plucked from the tea bushes throughout the year are transformed into tea, one of Sri Lanka's most famous exports. Just outside Ratnapura, you come to an unmarked fork. Both roads lead to Ratnapura, but the broader road in front is better and one of the few stretches in Sri Lanka where your car can safely pick up speed.

When you arrive, head straight for the **Ratnapura Rest House** (Tel: 052-2299) about ½ mile (1km) past the bus stand up Hill Road. Turn left and follow the signs. Have a wash and order lunch for 1pm, which gives you time to browse around Ratnapura. There is a selection of stones at the Rest House's gem shop if you're interested. Drive back to the bus stand, turn left and go about a mile (1.6km) to **Council Avenue**, and a large spacious

Tea for two

ground where gem dealers sell natural stones, uncut without the glitter of polished gems.

Turn left and travel about ½ mile (1km) on Council Avenue to Pothgul Vihare Road. Incredibly, there are no signs on this road as to where to turn to Pothgul Vihare so after about 3 miles (5km), turn right where you see the sign to Rajasilagama to visit a **gem mine** before the workers finish for the day at 1pm.

54

Park the car and climb up to the sound of a motor pumping out water. At the gem mine, see a pit about 12ft (4m) deep where soil containing pre-Cambrian gravel is dug out. Men dressed in skimpy loincloths work to bring the alluvial soil from the gem mine to the surface. Nearby, the soil is washed using a large wicker basket with a large rim. As the lighter sand gets washed off, the heavier stones fall to the bottom. The man brings up the basket and, after a short

prayer, begins to sort through the stones. There is eager expectation in the eyes of all watching. But not all are lucky: some end up millionaires while others remain as paupers.

After all that glitter, it's time to reflect on life's simpler virtues. The steep climb up 450 steps to **Pothgul Vihare** temple, built by King Valagambahu (89–77BC), begins here. As there is no water at the top, take some with you. You will need it by the time you reach the top and take in the spectacular scenery of the surrounding hills.

The temple has a massive rock forming the roof. There are two caves with old paintings and a statue of a reclining Buddha. Unlike most other temples, it is possible to go round to the back of the statue and have a good look. Outside is a sculpture of a devil with his mouth open and on top of the rock, a figure ready to jump in. This depicts one of the 550 lives of the Buddha, where he sacrifices himself by jumping into the mouth of a devil.

From rock to finished product

Climb down and return to the Ratnapura Rest House, freshen up after the hot and sweaty climb and have lunch.

Visit the tranquil **Hotel Kalavati**, (Tel: 045-2465) about 4 miles (6km) from the Rest House on the Polhengoda Road. This 25-acre (10-ha) property offers peace, quiet amidst luxuriant vegetation to reflect on life. If you are interested in *ayurveda*, the natural system of medicine using herbs, the art is practised and there are three special herbal baths designed to treat specific ailments such as rheumatism or persistent headaches. Don't miss seeing the controversial Tantric statue.

Return to Ratnapura and travel 1 mile (1.6km) on

Polishing gem stones

the Badulla Road to the sign that directs you to Ehelapola Mawatha in the village of **Batugedera**. The interesting **Gemmological Museum** (open daily 8.30am–5.30pm, Tel: 045-2398) of Mr A G B Amarasinghe charges no entrance fee. Exhibits include different types of natural rocks from all over the world as well as gems found in Sri Lanka. Gem cutters show how precious stones are cut and polished on machines to a lustre. Have refreshments in the museum cafeteria before returning to Colombo.

11. Southern Coast Escapade

Drive through a region of remarkable diversity. Shop for local wares; see toddy tappers and visit a mask factory; observe the ocean's marvels in a glassbottom boat, see stilt fishermen, or simply laze the day away on a sandy cove. Although this tour can be done in a day, you will probably want to take it easy and linger a few days at one of the many beach resorts.

The southern coast is the most popular of Sri Lanka's beach resorts. The beaches are sandier than those on the west and do not shelve steeply into the sea. The eastern coast, where the sand and water is beautiful, is unfortunately not accessible to tourists due to the war with Tamil guerrillas. The south of Sri Lanka is prosperous and beautiful with a variety of beaches, hill country, wildlife and plantations of tea, rubber and coconut. A day is not enough to see everything, but let's try.

Getting to the south is easy. Take the Galle Road, which hugs the coast past Mount Lavinia (see *Itinerary 6*). Little of the sea is actually visible until Moratuwa, about 13 miles (21km) from Colombo.

At **Wadduwa**, little stalls sell reed baskets, coir and straw mats with eye-catching designs, brooms, brushes, basketware and bamboo lamp shades. Stop and have a look. Piles of *mangosteens*, a succulent creamy-fleshed fruit, are for sale throughout the year at **Kalutara**, 28 miles (45km) out of Colombo, though the price varies from season to season. Although *mangosteens* are

South Coast vistas

The Kalutara dagoba

plentiful throughout the island, Kalutara is reputed to have the best quality. Be careful not to get the reddish-brown juice of the *mangosteen* shell on your clothes as the sap stains indelibly.

Drive over the two bridges. If not for the convenient island in the middle, this would have been one very long bridge across the **Kalu Ganga River**. On the other side is the white **Kalutara** dagoba. Every vehicle driven by a Buddhist stops here without fail so that the driver can drop a coin into the till outside the temple to ensure a safe journey. Do the same for luck. The *dagoba* is unusual in that it is hollow inside with a smaller *stupa* in the centre of the hollow space. Look closely at the walls of the interior which are lined with paintings depicting the lives of the Buddha. As the *dagoba* is hollow and dome-shaped, words spoken by those standing on the other side can be heard quite clearly. There is also the bonus of magnificent views of the bridges and ocean beyond.

Just past Kalutara, to the right, is a pleasant hotel with lovely gardens called **Sinbad** but the approach road needs repair and the beach is virtually non-existent. The hotel also offers watersports on the lagoon of the Kalu Ganga.

Pass Katukurunda, an abandoned British airstrip now used for motorcycle and car races. Just past the 31st mile post (50km), there is a view of the sea, beach and coconut trees that will take your breath away. The full beauty of the island unfolds from here onwards. If you are puzzled by the ropes connecting the coconut trees, a man walking along it high above soon solves the mystery.

These are the high-wire *toddy* tappers, who tap the flower of the coconut for sap to make *toddy*, an alcoholic beverage. *Toddy* is big business in Sri Lanka as it is a popular drink among the working class male. The sap is also used to produce treacle and *jaggery*, a kind of brown sugar.

Drive through **Beruwela**, at 35 miles (56km), a fishing town dominated by Muslims, evidenced by many mosques. Past Alutgama is the beautiful holiday resort of **Bentota**, at 40 miles (64km). It is fronted by a lovely beach that is calm except during the monsoon season. October through April are the best months for swimming. Stop at the recently refurbished 81-room **Hotel Ceysands** (Tel: 034-75073) on the right, after crossing the Bentota river on the hotel ferry. Or visit the 135-room **Bentota Beach Hotel** (Tel: 034-75176), another

A prize catch from the deep seas

lovely complex built on the site of an old Portuguese fort with a large garden and natural rock swimming pool. Near the sandy beach, with rock pools fringed with coconut trees, you might see the hotel elephant. Non-residents can get a ride, though the mahout expects at least Rs 100.

If you are fortunate, you may chance upon fishermen hauling in their daily catch. Chanting 'Odi, helai, helai laam', to the resonant screech of seagulls, the fishermen tug at the nets, pulling them in. No one will object if you give a hand. Once the nets are in, the slippery heaps of fish are quickly gathered and divided amongst themselves.

The late Bevis Bawa's beautiful 5-acre (2-ha) private garden called **Brief** (open daily 9am–5pm) at Kalawila, is open to visitors. To get there, turn right at Alutgama along the Matugama Road just before reaching Bentota. After 3 miles (5km) past Dharga Town, turn left at Ambagaha Handiya (Mango Tree Junction) and turn right at the mosque after ½ mile (1km). Follow the signs which indicate 'To Brief' and at the sign that announces 'Short cut to Brief', turn right.

This road is better than the normal route but remember to take a sharp right where it indicates 'To Gardens'. A few yards up the hill you will come to the imposing gates. Drive in till you reach the house. Ring the bell and wait for someone to turn up. The gardens are well laid out and a fee of Rs 60 per visitor is charged.

Bevis, who served in the army, and was the tallest man in Sri Lanka, left his estate to his staff who valiantly try to maintain his standards. After visiting the gardens, ask the caretaker, Mr de Silva, to show you the house with its antiques. He may even show you the 7-ft (2.1-m) bed which Bevis, who was over 6ft (1.8m) tall, slept in.

His brother, Geoffrey, Sri Lanka's foremost architect, also has a garden in Bentota called *Lunuganga*, which, unfortunately, is not open to visitors. Author Robin Maughan in his book about the garden, describes *Lunuganga* as 'paradise, a shangrila, a glimpse of *nirvana*'. The sprawling house in the middle of this oasis houses many fine antique furniture, several of Bevis' paintings as well as the works of George Keyt and the late painter, Donald Friend.

Proceed along the coast to **Kosgoda**, where in addition to the hotels, there are turtle hatcheries. Take a break at **Triton Hotel** (Tel: 09-54041), at the 50th mile post (80km), the island's only

A Donald Friend painting at Brief

five-star beach property. The tall coconut trees have been left intact in the driveway and the lobby opens out into a vast blue expanse of one of two swimming pools and the stunning beach.

After lunch, stop at **Ambalangoda**, famous for its wide choice of masks and puppets. Just before the 53rd mile post (85km), prior to the turn-off on the left, is the **Ariyapala's mask factory**. Mainly used in devil dancing with grotesque movements, the colourful masks produced here usually have large protruding eyes and big teeth. Pick up a mask or two as souvenirs.

Drive through Ambalangoda town to **Hikkaduwa**, where an unchecked tourism boom has led to an indiscriminate rash of hotels on the beach.

Continue your journey to **Galle**, located 72 miles (116km) from Colombo. The main landmark here is the beautifully preserved 90-acre (36-ha) **Dutch fort**. Turn in towards the old gateway, whose walls are 45ft (14m) thick and are strong enough to withstand cannon balls.

Above the gateway is the coat of arms of Great Britain and Ireland. Inside, carved on stone is the monogram

Galle

VOC, which stands for 'Vereenigde Oost Indische Compagnie – Dutch East Indies Company'.

More than 300 years old, the monogram has two lions on either side and a cock perched on a rock as the crest. A walk along the ramparts reveals the amazing sewerage system devised by the Dutch. At high tide the sewers are cleared whilst the ebb carries away the discharge at low tide.

Within the fort are several important churches, including the oldest Protestant church in Sri Lanka, the **Groote Kerk**. Visit the **New Orient Hotel** (Tel: 09-22059) inside the Fort, where a valiant battle is being fought by the Brohier family, owners of the hotel, to retain its charm. High ceilings, large easy chairs and a lovely garden at the back of the hotel give this tired-looking building a unique character.

Another hotel worth visiting is **Hotel Closenberg** (Tel: 09-32241), which was the residence of Captain Bailey, the agent of the P&O Company, in the mid 19th century. Today, it has 21 rooms and boasts a magnificent view. The historical **mansion** with a museum (Tel: 09-23214) on **Leyn Baan Street** inside the Fort is also worth visiting. Ask for the owner M H A Gaffar, a gem merchant, who charges no entrance fee.

Proceed along the Galle-Matara road and turn right to **Unawatuna** beach, one of the nicest on the island. The sand stretches out lazily for miles and there is no shortage of space. Return to the main road and travel to **Koggala**. Here, an abandoned airstrip on the left became the island's third Investment Promotion Zone in the middle of 1991.

During the last part of the journey, visit **Weligama**, 90 miles (145km) along the Galle-Matara road. It's a very pleasant drive and the little sandy bays with coconut trees growing right beside the sea have adorned Airlanka's overseas advertisements for years. Between Ahangama and Weligama is the home of **stilt fishermen** who sit patiently fishing on sticks driven into the sea-bed. It's an exercise which does not seem fruitful, but try telling that to the fishermen! Stop to take pictures of this unusual sight.

After some refreshments at the **Weligama Bay Inn** (Tel: 041-5299) listening to the roar of the sea, an island just across from the inn will catch your eye. This is **Galduwa** (Rock Island). Known to some as Yakinige Dowa, 'She-Devil's Island', this garden isle was bought by Count de Mauny, a French expatriate in the 1930s. The Count converted the island into an exquisite garden, enclosing a nine-room octagonal jewel-like mansion decorated with eclectic handicrafts. The mansion is partially hidden by the shrubs and if the tide is low, walk across up to the little jetty.

On your return trip to Colombo, stop at a convenient spot to see the sun set into the sea, a spectacular Sri Lankan sight from any vantage point. With so many beaches to pick from, it is highly unlikely that you will want to return to Colombo so soon.

12. Wildlife at Yala

Sri Lanka is elephant country but the population is fast dwindling. Spend a night in Yala National Park in search of this magnificent mammal and the elusive leopard. This excursion can be done from Colombo or as an extension of Itinerary 11.

Established in 1899, **Yala National Park** in the south is recommended because there is a wide variety of species to be seen in the 500-sq mile (1,295-sq km) sanctuary. Hire a four-wheel drive vehicle from Colombo or go by taxi and hire a jeep locally at Tissamaharama. The latter is more convenient and less expensive. Book your accommodation at **Yala Safari Beach Hotel** from the agents, Jetwing Hotels Ltd of 457A Union Place, Colombo 2 (Tel: 698818). A room is about US$20 per night.

If starting your journey from Colombo, plan to leave about 7am and head south on the Colombo-Galle-Matara road. Continue along the coast 122 miles (195km) to **Tangalla**. Have lunch at the **Tangalla Bay Hotel** (Tel: 047-40346) on the right just before the town. Swimming is not recommended, but the view is beautiful from this hotel modelled after a ship.

From Tangalla, go south 27 miles (43km) to Hambantota. The lush low vegetation gives way to thorny plants and small shrubs, typical vegetation of the dry zone. Continue 16 miles (26km) on the main road along the coast which gradually turns inland towards **Tissamaharama**.

For those travelling from any of the southern coast resorts, follow Galle Road to Galle, then go along the coast to Matara and Hambantota. Follow the main road until you reach Tissamaharama.

Turn right into town, and as you will need a jeep for the excursion to the Yala National Park, stop to arrange for one. Sumedha Wanniarachchi of Singha Lanka Tours at the Tissamaharma Resthouse (Tel: 047-37299/37176) will help get you a vehicle for about Rs 1,200 per trip. Ask them to come to the Yala Safari Beach Hotel at 2.30pm that afternoon and the next morning at 5.30am.

To get to the hotel, drive along the lonely Kirinda road with the beautiful Tissa Maha Seya Dagoba on your left.

About 7 miles (11km) later, turn right at the Yala sign post. Drive on the gravel track for about 3 miles (5km), past the entrance to the National Park and on to the **Yala Safari Beach Hotel**, an isolated

Deer grazing undisturbed

property amidst shrub jungle close to the sea. Check in, have a cool drink and wait for the jeep to arrive.

Entry hours to the Park are between 5.45am and 3.30pm, although all visitors are allowed to stay in the park till 6.30pm. The entrance fee is Rs 50, and the tracker assigned by the Park has to be paid Rs 175. Most of them are experienced in the jungle and its ways and should prove very interesting companions. There is a small museum near the entrance which is worth seeing, but leave it for the next day if there is no time.

The tracker will show you places where animals can be found. Very often, these will be near water holes where the animals come to drink in the evening and early morning. There are wild boars, wild buffaloes, crocodiles, sambars, monkeys, flying squirrels and a wide variety of birds including ducks which migrate from India and even as far away as Europe, to be seen.

It's a wonderful sight to see herds of deer, sometimes 60 to 100 strong, grazing or just gazing. Painted storks, herons, ibis and egrets abound. But definitely the greatest thrill is seeing wild elephants and leopards. The elephant found in Sri Lanka belongs to the same sub-species found throughout Asia. The elephants move majestically and are seldom bothered about visitors except if they feel threatened.

Leopards are rare at Yala and spotting one can be the highlight

of your adventure. A persistent tracker often finds one, sometimes seen playing like an overgrown cat on the road. Keep a look out for the magnificent spotted leopard which, though widely distributed throughout the island, is not easily seen due to its nocturnal habits.

Return to the hotel at dusk, wash off the dust and retire early after dinner. The jeep will be back early next

On the way to Yala

morning for another day. After another tour of the Park, return to the hotel about 9am for breakfast and stroll down to the beach to visit a colony of migratory fishermen who have pitched their huts here. They lead a nomadic life, moving from place to place wherever the fishing is bountiful.

Leave for Colombo and return to the Tissamaharama-Kirinda Road and turn right. At **Kirinda** there is a lovely view of the southern coast from a temple atop a rock. Here landed Viharamahadevi, the mother of the great hero of the Sinhala people, Dutugemunu. She had been sacrificed by her father, King Kelanitissa of Kelaniya to placate angry gods who were blamed for sea erosion.

Return to Colombo along the same road and stop for lunch at the **Dickwella Village Resort** (Tel: 041-2961) at 102 miles (164 km), a lovely Italian-style beach resort just before Matara.

13. The Ruined Cities of the North

A two-day excursion into Sri Lanka's past. Visit the historic sites of Dambulla, Polonnaruwa, Sigiriya and Anuradhapura.

An overnight trip to the island's ancient historical sites — or what Sri Lankans call the ruined cities — is a worthwhile expedition. Dating back more than 2,500 years, some of the sites are better preserved than others. A two-day trip can encompass Dambulla, Polonnaruwa, Sigiriya and Anuradhapura.

Kurunegala district

The engineering skills of these early Sri Lankans is something to marvel at. Where else in the world but at Sigiriya would you find water gardens built atop solid rock 1,500 years ago?

A recent attempt to divert the island's longest river, the Mahaweli, had overseas experts studying contours and water flow for months, using computers and complicated scientific instruments. Concluding that a major diversion should be made at Minipe, they found to their amazement evidence of a similar attempt made over a thousand years ago!

A permit to visit all the four sites costs US$28 but individual permits for each site costs US$10. Children between 8 and 12 pay half the price. The tickets, including a permit to take photographs can be obtained either at the respective sites or in Colombo from the Cultural Triangle Fund, 212 Bauddhaloka Mawatha, Colombo 7 (Tel: 587912, 500733).

Dambulla Cave Temple

Depart early in the morning at 6am to reach Dambulla by 10am to see the rock caves which close from 11am to 2pm. Take the Colombo-Kandy Road and turn left to Kurunegala at the signpost. Take the Dambulla Road from Kurunegala, 58 miles (93km) from Colombo. At Dambulla, 93 miles (150km) from Colombo, turn right on Kandy Road. The rock caves are on the right soon after passing the Dambulla Rest House on the left.

The **Dambulla Cave Temple**, the most impressive of Sri Lanka's many cave temples is a must. King Valagambahu fled here from Anuradhapura in the 1st century BC when South Indian Tamils captured the capital. After regaining his capital, the king built a temple in the caves where he had hidden. But it was King Nissankamalla of Polonnaruwa who gilded the interior of the caves, which later became known as Rangiri (Gold Rock) Dambulla. There are five caves and the 350-ft (107-m) climb to the temple is well worth it. The very first cave is the smallest but has a 45-ft (14-m) reclining Buddha carved out of rock. The second has a mini *dagoba* surrounded by Buddha statues, some carved out of the rock wall.

Unfortunately, some of the frescoes depicting the lives of the Buddha are in a state of decay and restoration work is going on. As if guarding his interests, there is a statue of King Valagambahu standing watch over the 100 Buddha statues and Hindu gods.

Freshen up and have drinks at the **Dambulla Rest House** (Tel: 066-8299) run by the Ceylon Hotels Corporation. Return to the Colombo-Anuradhapura-Kandy road junction and turn right to Habarana and then right again towards Polonnaruwa. There are no signposts at Habarana to indicate where to turn but there is a police station at the junction. The Habarana-Polonnaruwa stretch is one of the loneliest in this area and it is not unusual to see wild animals, including deer, monkeys and iguanas. The road is good but watch out for jagged edges and unmarked bends.

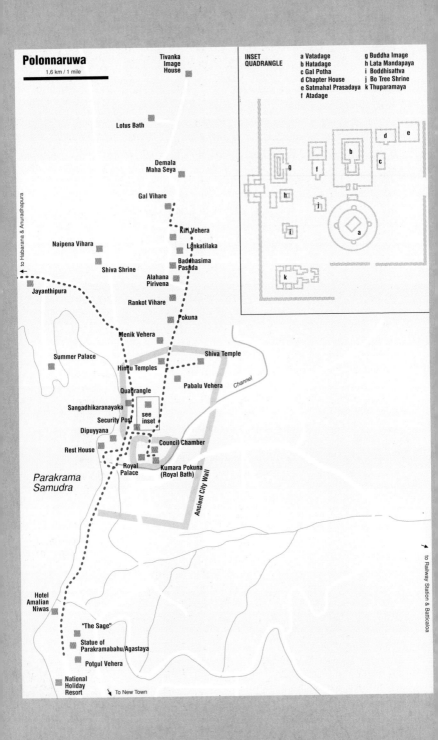

Polonnaruwa

1,6 km / 1 mile

INSET QUADRANGLE

a Vatadage
b Hatadage
c Gal Potha
d Chapter House
e Satmahal Prasadaya
f Atadage

g Buddha Image
h Lata Mandapaya
i Boddhisattva
j Bo Tree Shrine
k Thuparamaya

Tivanka Image House

Lotus Bath

Demala Maha Seya

Gal Vihare

Kiri Vehera

Lankatilaka

Baddhasima Pasada

Alahana Pirivena

Rankot Vihare

Pokuna

Menik Vehera

Shiva Temple

Hindu Temples

Pabalu Vehera

Channel

Quadrangle

Sangadhikaranayaka

see inset

Security Post

Dipuyyana

Council Chamber

Rest House

Royal Palace

Kumara Pokuna (Royal Bath)

Parakrama Samudra

Naipena Vihara

Shiva Shrine

Jayanthipura

Summer Palace

to Habarana & Anuradhapura

Ancient City Wall

to Railway Station & Batticaloa

Hotel Amalian Niwas

"The Sage"

Statue of Parakramabahu/Agastaya

Potgul Vehera

National Holiday Resort

To New Town

Providing precious irrigation water

Polonnaruwa was at its zenith of power and glory in the 11th century but the capital city lasted only 200 years. Under its most illustrious king, Parakramabahu I (1153–86), this was the only era during which rice was exported and Sri Lankans ventured overseas.

A mile (1.6km) before the town, the ruins suddenly come into view on the left. As it would be approaching lunchtime, continue another mile (1.6km) and turn right towards the Rest House. The **Parakrama Samudra** (Ocean of Parakrama) lies before you, a vast reservoir of water covering 6,000 acres (2,430ha). The amazing King Parakramabahu who built the tank proclaimed that not one drop of water should escape into the ocean without it being of some service to man.

Today, the reservoir is the lifeblood of the region, as it was in ancient times, providing precious irrigation water for some 18,200 acres (7,365ha) of paddy land. Along the bund, about 1½ miles (2km) is **Hotel Amalian Niwas** (Tel: 027-2405), where you can order lunch. While it is being prepared, drive ½ mile (1km) along the road to a controversial statue carved on a rock. Depending on the source, this is either King Parakramabahu or Agastaya, an Indian religious teacher.

Return to have lunch and then drive up to the ancient ruins. Tickets are checked at a security post or can be purchased here for US$10 if you have not bought them earlier.

King Parakramabahu's **Royal Palace** is to the right. Of the original seven floors, only three remain. A staircase leads to nowhere but the former grandeur can be imagined. The brick walls have large holes for the giant beams of the ceiling. Ancient books tell of a lift to transport those who worked at the palace to the top floors.

In front of the Royal Palace is the administrative building and audience hall which have been restored by the British. Some fine

Polonnaruwa dagoba from a distance

Royal Palace ruins

specimens of elephant carvings have been preserved but even the best craftsmen make mistakes. No prize is offered for those who discover the five-legged elephant near one of the entrances. Notice the interesting change in the moonstones, the semi circular works of art which are found near entrances to important buildings. Unlike the Anuradhapura moonstones that you will see tomorrow, the ox has gone from the design, a change attributed to Hindu influence which considers the ox sacred.

Nearby is a lovely tree with a natural cavity, ideal for children to hide in. Just below are the remains of the walls and the royal bath, **Kumara Pokuna**. It is a large but exquisite stepped bath of cut stone. Underground stone conduits feed it with water from the Parakrama Samudra. However, only two of the original five crocodile spouts for water are well preserved.

Drive back to the security post and turn right down the gravel path. As the reign in Polonnaruwa was brief, most of the important ruins are confined to a smaller area compared to Anuradhapura. About a mile (1.6km) down this road, there is a lonely post to the left. This is the **Sangadhikaranayaka** (The Court of the Monks), where Buddhist monks who indulged in bad behaviour were held after trial by their peers. They were then defrocked and banished to a village called Hiraluwa to become farmers. To this day, a monk who has left his robes is called a *hiraluwa* by the Sinhala people.

Try a coconut at the nearby refreshment stand. After drinking the water, the vendor will split the coconut open. Eat part of the flesh and throw the remainder to the monkeys. Their agility is incredible as they jump to catch what you offer.

Two stalls sell souvenirs. **M Chandrasekera's**, closer to the coconut vendors, has some lovely wooden cars made of ebony and some artificially-aged statues of Buddha and Hindu gods.

A number of ruins are concentrated in the **Quadrangle**. Climb the steps to the **Sathmahal Prasadaya** (Seven-storey *Dagoba*) on the right. Its former seven floors show a distinct Burmese influ-

Sathmahal Prasadaya

ence, a country with whom Parakramabahu established links.

Next is the massive 30-ft (9-m) long **Gal Potha** (Rock Book), one of the longest and heaviest books in the world. The enormous slab of stone is 5ft (1½m) wide and over 2ft (60cm) thick. The rock is inscribed with the great achievements of Parakramabahu's successor and nephew, Nissankamalla, who in a hurry to outdo his uncle, indulged in an orgy building monuments and temples.

An interesting footnote shows that the Gal Potha Rock Book was brought from Mihintale, over 60 miles (97km) away. The 25-ton (25-kg) book was believed to have been transported to its present site on wooden rollers by elephants.

Nearby is the **Hatadage**, where the tooth of the Buddha was once enshrined. Built by King Nissankamalla, a close study of the columns reveal some erotic carvings. To prevent destruction by Tamil Hindu adventurers, the King had bulls carved at the entrance, but to no avail.

Gal Potha makes for heavy reading

Next is the **Atadage**, built by King Parakramabahu's predecessor, King Vijayabahu, which at one time also housed the Buddha's tooth. The altar opposite the Buddha image was believed to be where King Nissankamalla sat, listening to Buddhist discourses.

The **Thuparamaya** is the only building with a roof over it. This temple contains nine statues of the Buddha. One is broken while others glisten magically under the light as they are made of quartz and contain mica. Light a candle and the wonders of Thuparamaya are revealed. One statue is believed to have had gems embedded as eyes which emitted strange rays when sunlight streaked in from specially constructed angled crevices.

The **Vatadage** has no roof but is a beautiful circular relic house constructed by King Parakramabahu. It is probably the oldest building in Polonnaruwa, preceding by several centuries the establishment of the capital. Do not be deceived by the inscription made by King Nissankamalla claiming he constructed it. Politicians taking credit for what they have not done is an old trait.

There are four entrances at compass points, leading to four Buddha statues and a central *dagoba*. One of the statues is broken but the grandeur of the place remains intact, despite there being no roof. The main entrance has a well preserved rock moonstone flanked by two guardstones.

Beyond the Vatadage is the **Shiva Temple** where the *yoni* and

lingum, symbols of fertility, are worshipped by Hindu women seeking blessings for conception. Remember to remove your shoes and headgear before entering.

Continuing your journey by car, the **Rankot Vihare** (Golden Pinnacle) is on the left, a *dagoba* 125-ft (38-m) high with a circumference of 550ft (168m). The remains of the **Alahana Pirivena** (university) and the **royal burial grounds** are nearby.

Drive on to a car park with some souvenir stalls and alight to visit the well preserved **Kiri Vehera** (Milk *Dagoba*) and the image house, **Lankatilaka**, with its 56-ft (17-m) thick walls and the headless statue of the standing Buddha.

Cross the road and walk to the **Gal Vihare** (Rock Temple) where some of the finest examples of 11th-century craftsmen are the four Buddha statues carved out of sheer rock. Disciple Ananda stands beside the Buddha, arms folded and one leg bent in the *Tivanka* posture. The most detailed and impressive statue is the 43-ft (13-m) reclining Buddha. Note the slight depression in the pillow under his head, and the marks on the soles of his feet.

The seated Buddha in deep meditation is under an arch and beside him, in a cave, is a smaller Buddha with his attendants. On the left of the cave are the frescoes, still in their original colours, which once adorned the walls.

There is more to see in Polonnaruwa but by now it will be about time to leave. Return to the car and the Habarana Road. About 3 miles (5km) from Polonnaruwa, stop in **Jayanthipura** at the **Pubudu Lace Centre**, an open building on the left. Beautiful lace souvenirs are for sale, including table mats, table cloths, curtains and pillow cases as well as some batik dresses.

Spend the night at **The Village** (Tel: 066-8316) in **Habarana**, a lovely property with a swimming pool, gardens and rooms in separate chalets. A short walk away is the lake where a hotel boat is available. My favourite, though, is the giant chess board with pieces as high as a child. If there is no room at The Village, try the more up-market **Lodge** (Tel: 066-8321) run by the same hotel group. The rooms are larger and suitable for families. One of the joys of these hotels is the sounds of the jungle and the grunts of wild animals at night. Enjoy gazing at stars in a clear sky and reflect on what you have seen during the day.

Next morning, leave about 7am for Sigiriya in order to avoid climbing in the heat of noon. Turn right at The Village gate and after about 16 miles (26km), turn left at the Sigiriya signboard, just past the 98th mile post (158km). The entrance fee is US$10 if you do not already have the ticket. On the approach road, watch out for monkeys in the old fortifications on the right.

Sigiriya was built by King Kassapa (AD447–495), after the model of Mount Kailas, home of the gods. Kassapa had killed his father in search of wealth and then chased his brother, Moggalana, to India. Though Sigiriya palace was impregnable, Kassapa met his doom on the plains.

Hearing that his brother had raised an army and was coming to wage war, Kassapa set out with his army to surprise them. When he turned his elephant round to outflank them and to avoid a marsh, his men misunderstood the action. They thought he had given up the fight and ran away. Kassapa, in panic, committed suicide.

Kassapa's palace is built on top of a huge rock, rising about 650ft (198m), and the only access is through the mouth of a lion whose likeness was once carved halfway up the monolith – hence the name Sigiriya (**Lion Rock**). A moat filled with crocodiles once guarded the entrance. The pleasure gardens at the foot of the rock are being excavated and restored by UNESCO.

Look for Cecil Weerakoon at the entrance. He is an excellent guide who has spent 35 years with the Archaeological Department.

A brick stairway and then a spiral staircase leads you to the **Art Gallery**, which once housed 500 frescoes of heavenly maidens. Today, only about 18 of these frescoes remain, but you see even less as one section of the Gallery is closed. But what is on show is enough to delight the eye.

Sigiriya, the 'Lion Rock' monolith

Voluptuous, bare bodied maidens holding baskets of flowers seem to float among clouds. No one knows whether the seductive beauties – painted in tempera in brilliant colours on the rock wall – were meant to be goddesses, Kassapa's concubines or dancers, but the sophisticated use of colour and form over 1,500 years ago expresses the level of artistry attained.

Climb past the **Mirror Wall** which once doubled the frescoes with its reflections. Try to ignore the old and new graffiti. Halfway up, there is a refreshment stall where prices are triple the normal rate. This is not unreasonable as drinks have to be carried a great distance to the stall.

The final climb to the top is on a crude staircase cut into the rock with a handrail. Called **Lion Terrace**, it is bounded on three sides by a low parapet, with a sheer cliff cutting down from the fourth (south) side. One can only imagine the intimidating military advantage this city must have had when the enemy had to go into this one path through the jaws of the menacing beast.

You would have to climb through two clawed paws to reach the steep stairwell. This climb is not for the faint-hearted but for those who venture forth, the view encompasses breathtaking scenery. Unfortunately, only the foundations are visible but the pool cut into the rock, 88ft by 68ft (27m by 21m), makes one wonder what a massive workforce was needed to create this tremendous fortress.

Go back to the main road and stop briefly at the **New Gamini Ebony Workshop** to see local wood craftsmen at work. Among the items that will catch your eye are jewellery boxes inlaid with porcupine quills for about Rs 1,250. Take a short break at Sigiriya Village, a 25-acre (10-ha) resort.

Once refreshed, take the Sigiriya-Anuradhapura Road, stopping for a quick lunch at the **Tissawewa Rest House** (Tel: 025-2299) before proceeding to Anuradhapura.

There are many things to see at Sri Lanka's first capital, founded by King Pandukhabaya in 380BC. Unlike Polonnaruwa's brief and uncomplicated history, **Anuradhapura** remained as the island's capital for over 1,400 years, before pressure from the Tamils of South India finally forced it to move eastwards.

In 247BC, Mahinda, the son of Emperor Ashoka of India, helped Pandukhabaya's grandson, King Devanampiyatissa, to become a Buddhist. This led to a hive of building activity. Gathering merit through performance of merito-

Buddhist offerings

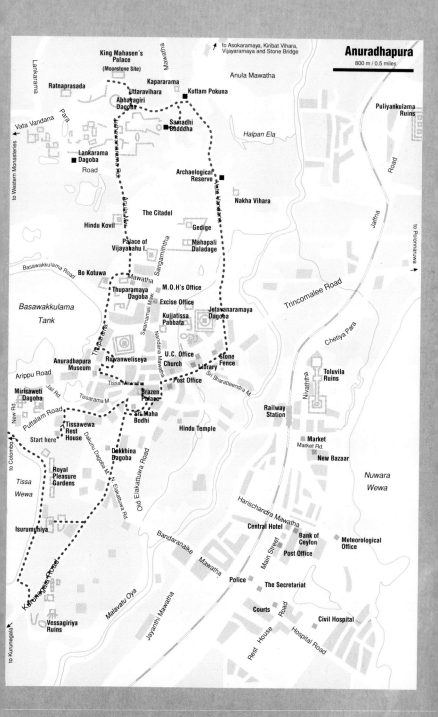

Anuradhapura

800 m / 0.5 miles

to Asokaramaya, Kiribat Vihara, Vijayaramaya and Stone Bridge

King Mahasen's Palace (Moonstone Site)

Ratnaprasada

Kapararama

Anula Mawatha

Uttaravihara

Kuttam Pokuna

Abhayagiri Dagoba

Puliyankulama Ruins

Vata Vandana

to Western Monasteries

Samadhi Buddha

Lankarama Dagoba

Road

Archaelogical Reserve

Nakha Vihara

Halpan Ela

The Citadel

Hindu Kovil

Gedige

Palace of Vijayabahu I.

Mahapali Daladage

Basawakkulama Road

Bo Kotuwa

Mawatha

Thuparamaya Dagoba

M.O.H's Office

Trincomalee Road

Excise Office

Chetiya Para

Basawakkulama Tank

Kujjatissa Pabbata

Jetavanaramaya Dagoba

Toluvila Ruins

Anuradhapura Museum

Ruwanweliseya

U.C. Office Church

Aruppu Road

Tissa Mawatha

Post Office

Stone Fence

Library

Railway Station

Nivaththa

Mirisaweti Dagoba

Jail Rd.

Tissarama M.

Brazen Palace

Sri Maha Bodhi

Hindu Temple

Market

Market Rd.

New Bazaar

Nuwara Wewa

Start here

Tissawewa Rest House

Dekkhina Dagoba

Royal Pleasure Gardens

Tissa Wewa

Harischandra Mawatha

Central Hotel

Bank of Ceylon

Meteorological Office

Post Office

Isurumuniya

Bandaranaike

Mawatha

Malavatu Oya

Police

The Secretariat

Courts

Civil Hospital

Vessagiriya Ruins

to Kurunegala

to Colombo

Jayanthi Mawatha

Main Street

Rest House Road

Hospital Road

rious acts is an important aspect of Buddhism, which is why so many *dagobas* and temples were constructed. As Anuradhapura is in the dry zone and storage of water in reservoirs is vital for agriculture, these people developed a tremendous knowledge of construction, water conservation and management.

Drive to the **Sri Maha Bodhi** or sacred *bo* tree, which grew from a sapling of the original *bo* tree of Bodhgaya in India under which the Buddha gained enlightenment. This is the oldest historically documented tree in the world, brought to Sri Lanka by Sangamitta, the daughter of Emperor Ashoka in 3rd century BC. Encircled by a gold-plated railing, it stands amidst other younger trees on a special platform, a *bodhigara*. Most of the island's *bo* trees have been nurtured from Maha Bodhi's seeds.

Watering the *bo* tree is considered an act of devotion by Buddhists and many pilgrims with pots of water in hand help nourish the plant. It is prohibited to pluck leaves but there is nothing to prevent you from picking up a fallen leaf as a souvenir.

Near the *bo* tree is the **Brazen Palace**, which once had a bronze roof, nine floors and 1,000 monks, with the most senior one occupying the top floor. How did he get there? By an elevator of course, according to historical records, though no other details are available. Only about 1,600 stone pillars now remain of what once must have been an imposing building.

Drive along the road between the tree and the palace to the **Anuradhapura Museum** (open daily 9am–5pm except Friday, Tel: 025-2589) which has many fine carvings of the Anuradhapura era and a model of the Thuparama Vatadage, complete with wooden roof.

At the entrance to the right is a statue of the man who spent a lifetime discovering the intricacies of an ancient civilization, Dr Senarath Paranavitarana. Among the interesting exhibits are female figures on guardstones, indicating that King Kassapa employed females as guards. There are agricultural implements, coins, pots and even impressions of a dog's paw and a man's toe on some bricks. Look at the museum's roof which resembles an umbrella.

Drive towards the north and see the **Ruwanweliseya**, a *dagoba* constructed by King Dutugemunu (161–137BC), the hero of the Sinhala race. It was he who liberated Anuradhapura from the Tamil yoke by defeating King Elara, but was so horrified by the destruction of life that he decided to devote his short lifetime to building

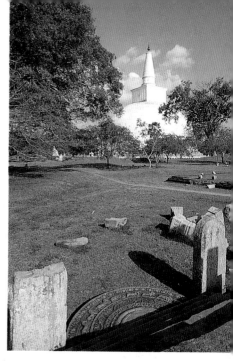

dagobas. Ruwanweliseya, over 500ft (152m) high with a 300-ft (90-m) dome, is his best-known construction, and regarded as the greatest of Anuradhapura's *dagobas.*

But Dutugemunu did not live to see the *dagoba* completed and the *Mahawamsa* describes how white cloth was draped round the semi-completed building for the dying king to see his greatest work. The wall has a frieze of elephants and the limestone statue is believed to be of King Dutugemunu.

Turn left and drive north to the **Thuparamaya**, the oldest *dagoba* on the island, believed to contain the right collar bone of the Buddha. It was constructed by King Devanampiyatissa and is only just over 60ft (18m) high. Erected entirely out of earth in the 3rd century BC, this *dagoba* was improved upon by successive rulers. Its present 'bell' shape is the result of restoration work in 1862.

Drive along Anula Mawatha, straight ahead to the **Abhayagiri Dagoba**, constructed by the ubiquitous King Valagambahu (89–77BC). This is 243ft (74m) high, though historical records indicate it was restored by King Parakramabahu who raised it to a height of 328ft (100m).

Turn left to **King Mahasen's Palace**. Among the ruins is the finest moonstone in Anuradhapura, cut on rock. A few yards up the road is the **Ratnaprasada**, built in the 8th century, with two of the best preserved guardstones of the Anuradhapura era. The *Naga* (Snake) king is seated under a *makara* arch, holding a flower pot and lotus stalk – two symbols that Sri Lankans associate with plenty and prosperity. Return to the Abhaya–giri *Dagoba*, turn right at the cross-road and drive straight down to the **Samadhi Buddha**, a fine example of sculpture from the 4th century.

Samadhi Buddha in repose

Return to the crossroad, turn right and visit the rectangular, connected twin ponds, the **Kuttam Pokuna**. According to records, the water supply was piped underground from 4 miles (6km) away and entered the smaller pond through the mouth of the *makara*, Sri Lanka's equivalent of the dragon. The **five-headed cobra**, now used

Tissawewa Tank

as a logo by the Board of Investment, can be seen near the *makara*.

Drive along the outer circular road (Vata Vandana) to the **Jetawanaramaya**, the largest *dagoba* in the world. Built by King Mahasen (AD273–303), it originally stood at over 400ft (122m) tall, with a diameter of 370ft (113m). Occupying some 8 acres (3.2ha) of land, the structure is a little smaller than the Great Pyramid of Egypt.

The final visit is to the **Isurumuniya** rock temple. To reach it, drive on the road south until you see the Brazen Palace on your right. Turn left soon after passing the *bo* tree and go south towards the **Tissawewa Tank**. Ascribed to King Devanampiyatissa in the 3rd century BC, he made it Anuradhapura's chief source of water.

Isurumuniya, built in the 3rd century BC as part of a monastic complex called Issiramana, is on the right. Here stands the famous 4th-century limestone carving of the Isurumuniya lovers, a man and a woman immortalised in song. The woman lifts a warning finger but the man carries on regardless. Some say that the figures represent Dutugemunu's son, Saliya and the low-caste maiden whom he loved.

As you climb up towards the cave containing a statue of the reclining Buddha cut from rock, note the sculpture of two elephants splashing water. Nearby is a carving in high relief of a man, probably of royal blood, with a horse looking over his shoulder.

The frisky Isurumuniya lovers

Return to Colombo via Puttalam along the western coast. At Anuradhapura, turn onto the A12, then zip along the coastal road to Chilaw, past Negombo and the international airport at Katunayake to Colombo.

Right: sunset at Anuradhapura

Calendar of Special Events

Sri Lanka has the dubious distinction of being known as the land with the largest number of official public holidays in the world, all 27 of them. The reason for this is that every major event in the Buddhist, Hindu, Muslim and Christian calendar is celebrated as a holiday on the island.

Apart from shops, entertainment houses and business establishments being closed, no liquor is served in hotels and restaurants on *Poya* (full moon) public holidays. If coming on a business visit, bear this in mind.

Kandy Perahera festival

The dates of major Buddhist Pereheras (processions) fluctuate annually and depend on the lunar calendar. Check specific dates in advance with the Sri Lankan High Commission or embassy in your country or the Ceylon Tourist Board office in Colombo (Tel: 437059, 437060).

JANUARY

Duruthu Perehera: The Kelaniya Temple near Colombo commemorates the visit of the Buddha to Kelaniya.
Thai Pongal: (14 January) A Hindu harvest festival of the Sun God.

FEBRUARY

Independence Day: (4 February) Marked with parades, dances, floats and other cultural events.
Navam Perehera: This celebration at the Gangarama Temple in Colombo is fast establishing itself on the tourist calendar as a must. Elephants and dancers parade for three nights.
Mahashivaratri: The Hindu festival which commemorates the winning of Lord Shiva by his consort, Parvati, through penance.

MARCH

Good Friday/Easter Sunday: Roman Catholics in Duwa, off Negombo to the west of Colombo present a passion play, similar to Oberammergau.

APRIL

Sinhala/Hindu New Year: (April 13–14) For the Sinhalese and the Tamils, the two main communities on the island, the New Year is an occa-

Devotees at Kataragama

sion for people to remember age-old traditions, boil auspicious milk rice, wear new clothes and visit their parents and loved ones. It is also a time for much merrymaking and games.

MAY

May Day: (May 1) Celebrated with huge rallies. In Colombo, one of the biggest shows is held at Galle Face Green, when the ruling UNP has a meeting followed by a musical show to which Indian stars are invited.

Wesak: The Buddhist celebration, commemorating the birthday, enlightenment and death of the Buddha. Homes are illuminated with bright lights and lanterns. Look out for pandals, bamboo frameworks hung with paintings illuminating various scenes of the lives of the Buddha.

It is also a time for dansal, or donation of food, and free meals and drinks are given throughout the island. The temples are usually filled with devotees paying their respects.

National Heroes Day: (22 May).

JUNE

Poson: Full moon day. Island-wide celebration of the arrival of Buddhism to Sri Lanka through the son of Emperor Ashoka of India.

JULY/AUGUST

Kataragama: The festival at this jungle shrine in southern Sri Lanka includes a Perehera (procession). Fire walking is also a traditional feature.

Kandy Perehera: This is one of the oldest historical pageants in the world, has been held for centuries and is the event of the year. The hills of Kandy come alive to the throbbing of drums, the tinkling bells of gaily caparisoned elephants and costumed Kandyan dancers. The Perehera goes on for 10 nights and ends with a water cutting ceremony. This involves using a sword to symbolically cut the waters of the Mahaweli River.

Water taken immediately from where the sword divides is contained in a special pot and kept in the Temple of the Tooth until the next Perehera. A replica of the Buddha's tooth is paraded through the streets on the back of an elephant.

Vel: During this Hindu festival, a Hindu cart is drawn by two massive bulls through the streets of Colombo.

NOVEMBER

Deepavali (Diwali): The triumph of light over darkness is celebrated with lights decorating Hindu homes to welcome Lakshmi, the goddess of wealth and prosperity.

DECEMBER

Christmas/New Year: (December 25/January 1) Celebrated throughout. The latter is heralded by thousands of fire crackers.

This is the beginning of the season to visit the holiest mountain in the world, **Adam's Peak**. The auspicious period is from December to March.

*In addition to the above festivals, Muslims also celebrate the end of the Ramadan fasting month, the Haj festival and the Birthday of Prophet Mohammed. The dates of these festivals vary from year to year.

Practical Information

By Air

Most visitors arrive by air at Colombo International Airport. Also known as Katunayake International Airport, it is located near the town of Katunayake, 20

miles (32km) north of Colombo city. There is no other major international airport on the island.

Airlanka (UL), the national carrier, provides service to and from Europe, the Middle East, India, Pakistan and East Asia. Singapore Airlines and Thai International offer services from USA and Australia.

By Sea

Cruise ships are no longer the main means of transportation to Sri Lanka, but a number of cruise lines still call at her ports. Each cruise line sets its own schedule according to customer demands. If you are interested in cruising to Sri Lanka, contact several travel agents and make arrangements through the one which has schedules and itineraries most appealing to you. Several liners stop on round-the-world-cruises (such as P & O Lines and the *Queen Elizabeth II*), while others (such as CTC) offer regional cruises.

Some freighters offer limited passenger space. Check directly with the shipping lines for this option.

When to Visit

For the west and south coast, the best months are November to March when the seas are calm and the weather is quite good, though there's no guarantee there won't be showers. This is called the winter season and coincides with the European winter, when accommodation rates are at their highest. December and January are popular months and unless you book ahead, hotel rooms are difficult to find. April to October are the best months to visit the east coast but as the troubles in the north sometimes spill over to the eastern province, tourists are not encouraged to go there.

Sri Lanka has two monsoons. From May to July the south-west monsoon brings rain to the west and south, while the north-east monsoon waters the north and east from November to January.

March and April are the hottest months but it is lovely in the hills. Finding accommodation in places like Nuwara Eliya can be difficult during these months.

Visas and Passports

Nationals from about 30 countries do not need visas for stays up to one month if arriving as tourists. Check with your travel agent as more countries are periodically added to the list. It is important to remember that no visas are given on arrival to those from countries not on the list. Visas should be obtained from a Sri Lankan Consular Office, or through a British Consular Office if there are no Sri Lankan Offices.

Visa extensions are given at the Department of Emigration and Immigration, Galle Buck Road, Colombo 1, Tel: 329851. The visa charge is usually the amount that the visitor's country charges for a Sri Lankan visiting that country. Proof of money spent in the country may be requested and it is best to be prepared with encashment certificates of foreign exchange.

Vaccinations

Yellow fever vaccinations are essential if coming from an infected country. Immunization against cholera and Hepatitis A is recommended. Anti-malaria pills are recommended if one is visiting the ancient cities.

Customs

Those bringing over US$5,000 should declare it at Customs on arrival. Valuable equipment, gems and jewellery should also be declared.

Tourists should go through the green channel if there is nothing to declare. Duty free allowances include 2 litres of spirits, two bottles of wine, 200 cigarettes or 50 cigars and a small quantity of perfume. Import of dangerous drugs, firearms, obscene literature and pictures is an offence. Illegal drug importers can be punished with death.

All bags are X-rayed and physically checked by security personnel at the Customs counter. Batteries, radios and electronic equipment are best checked in rather than hand carried. If gems have been purchased in Sri Lanka, it is best to keep the receipt to show to Customs if requested. Sri Lankan money can be reconverted at the departure lounge before checking in.

Climate

In Colombo, the average annual temperature is 27°C (81°F); in Kandy at an altitude of 1,000ft (305m) it is 20°C (68°F); and in Nuwara Eliya, nestled high in the hills at 6,200ft (1,890m), the temperature averages 16°C (61°F). The highest temperatures are usually reached between March and June, while November to January are the coolest months. But note that the difference between the 'hot' and 'cool' season is only a matter of a few degrees. The ocean, however, remains a constant 27°C (81°F) throughout the whole year.

Clothing

Casual wear of light cotton or terry cotton material is recommended but for the hill country, where temperatures in the night drop to 10°C (50°F) at times, a sweater is recommended. A good insect repellent and sunscreen lotion with a high Sun Protection Factor (SPF) is advised. The sun is hotter than one thinks and without adequate protection, sunburns due to long exposure, especially at beach resorts, can lead to an unpleasant holiday. Drink plenty of liquids as the heat and humidity causes you to lose water through perspiration

Electricity

Electricity is 230 volts at 50 cycles AC. Some hotels have 110 volt outlets for shavers. The plugs are normally the round type. A multi-socket plug will be helpful.

Time Differences

Sri Lanka is 5½ hours ahead of Greenwich Mean Time (GMT).

Although the country is predominantly Buddhist, with the Buddhist year beginning on April 13, the Western calendar is used in business and by the Government.

GETTING ACQUAINTED

Government and Economy

Sri Lanka is a parliamentary democracy with an elected executive President. There are 225 members of parliament who are elected on a complicated proportional voting system.

Muslim girl

Veddah

The base of the country is agriculture but rice imports continue. Incredibly, the island imports canned fish. Agricultural products, tea, rubber and coconut account for about a third of the island's exports, while the rest is mainly industrial.

The per capita income of the 17 million inhabitants is US$418. With free education and health care, the literacy rate is 88.6 percent, one of the highest in Asia, whilst the infant mortality rate is one of the lowest. Sri Lanka has a population of 17.2 million (estimate) with a population growth rate of 1.6 percent, the lowest in South Asia.

Religion

Buddhists constitute 69.3 percent of the population, while Hindus 15.5 percent, Muslims 7.6 percent, Christians 7.5 percent and other religions 0.1 percent.

Geography

The length of the island is 277 miles (445km) and the width is 140 miles (225km). Girdled by over 1,000 miles (1,600km) of coastline, the island has a total land area of 24,560 sq miles (63,610 sq km), about the same as Holland and Belgium combined. The highest mountain is Pidurutalagala (8,281ft/2,524m).

Sri Jayewardenapura Kotte is the administrative capital and Colombo, with a population of about 650,000 people, is the commercial capital.

Preparing for prayers

Culture and Customs

Sri Lankans are a very friendly and helpful people, but beware of touts trying to take advantage of tourists. Making friends is easy and do not be amazed if you are invited to a Sri Lankan home for a meal. The locals are not camera shy but will often ask you for a copy of the photograph.

When entering Buddhist or Hindu temples, please remove your shoes and headgear as a sign of respect. Ladies should not wear short skirts, shorts or see-through blouses when entering temples. Monks should not be touched; if you meet one and wish to show respect, raise both hands in a prayer-like manner to just below your chin. Always be sensitive to the local religious sensibilities.

MONEY MATTERS

Currency and Credit Cards

The Sri Lanka rupee is made up of 100 cents. Coins and dollars come in different denominations. At time of press, the exchange rate for the US dollar was Rs 49.00. Check the newspapers daily for bank rates, but use this only as a guide as the actual amount one receives is a little less, depending on the bank. Some banks charge a fee for changing travellers cheques, and it is best to check exchange rates and bank charges before changing money. Rates of exchange offered at hotels are generally lower than at banks.

Note that the country is moving rapidly towards a convertible rupee.

All the major credit cards are accepted at major establishments, although some shops shun the American Express Card because of high commission charges.

Tipping

All hotel bills have to be paid in foreign exchange. This is where proof of exchange at banks will be helpful in the form of receipts and encashment certificates.

Most hotels and restaurants add a 10 percent service charge and a 5 percent Business Turnover Tax (BTT). An additional tip can be left for the waiter if the service pleases you. Rs 10 per bag carried by porters is a good tip.

Airport Tax

A departure tax of Rs 500 per passenger is charged. If you are going to the airport to meet someone off a flight, access to the airport waiting area costs Rs 40.

Black Market

The black market rate is only a few cents more and not worth the risk, so use the banks or an official money changer.

Business Hours

Government offices are open from 8am to 4pm Monday to Friday, and private offices stay open until 5pm. Shops are open from 9am to 6pm on weekdays and on Saturdays.

Most banks are open from 9am to 1.30pm on weekdays but some have longer hours. Seylan Bank closes at 8pm and is also open on Saturday from 9am to 11am.

GETTING AROUND

Taxis

Taxis charge between Rs 12–15 per kilometre travelled while auto rickshaws cost about Rs 10. Yellow radio taxis are small Japanese cars with little space. The meters work and are reliable unlike in the Morris Minor taxis and auto rickshaws where a price should be agreed before commencing the journey.

Radio-controlled taxis, Ace Cabs (Tel: 501502) and Kangaroo Cabs (Tel: 502888) charge Rs 21 a kilometre travelled with a minimum charge of Rs 28.

Trains

Train services are reliable and the intercity expresses between cities are recommended. There are usually second and third class tickets available, and a limited number of services with first class tickets. Inquiries on details of train times and bookings can be made from the Fort Railway Station, Tel: 435838 or 421281.

Train fares are very reasonable. The 72-mile (116-km) journey from Colombo to Kandy on the intercity costs Rs 60 while a third class ticket on a normal train costs only half that price.

Buses

Public transport is believed to be the cheapest in the world, but is very basic. There are a few luxury buses plying routes. The bus fare from Colombo to Kandy is less than the third class fare by rail.

Cars

The best way to get around is to hire a hotel taxi or arrange a chauffeur-driven car through a travel agent. The latter is cheaper than a self-drive car.

Many Sri Lankan drivers lack basic road manners and though the mood in the country is generally relaxed, patience is not the greatest virtue of Sri Lankans behind the wheel. You will not be far wrong if you think bus and taxi drivers seem to keep their fingers permanently pressed on the horn. Unless you are a very patient, careful driver, driving is best left to the locals.

Private cars charge about Rs 12 a kilometre. Self-drive cars are available at about Rs 15 per kilometre, but a refundable deposit of Rs 5,000 up will be requested. Often, unlike in Western countries, the car is given with a virtually empty tank so you must fill up at the nearest petrol station. International driving licenses have to be registered at the Automobile Association office next to the Holiday Inn in Galle Face, Colombo 3, (Tel: 421528/9), before hiring a self-drive car.

Motorbikes

The adventurous may like to rent motorbikes. A wide selection of the latest models are available from Goldwing, 346 Deans Road, Colombo 10 (Tel: 685750).

Air-taxis and Helicopters

Cessna two-seater planes and five-seater Bell helicopters are available for hire. Flights are from the Ratmalana Airport. Contact Upali Aviation at 34 Galle Road, Colombo 3 (Tel: 328826 or 329399) for the Cessna, and John Keells Aviation and Mackinnons Travels Ltd, 4 Leyden Bastian Road, Colombo 1 (Tel: 329881) for the helicopter.

A 24-seater helicopter offers scheduled services to the south and various tourist attractions at reasonable rates. Contact Ace Airways (Pte) Ltd, Cargills Building, 30 Sir Baron Jayatilleke Mawatha, Colombo 1 (Tel: 447239).

ACCOMMODATION

Sri Lanka has about 9,500 hotel rooms, of which 2,200 in Colombo are in the five-star category. As it is difficult to list all properties, all the five-star hotels and a few of the cheaper options are listed. Five-star hotels charge about US$75 a night, single/double occupancy. Moderate hotels charge between US$30 and US$60.

All hotels include a 10 percent service charge and a 5 percent Business Turnover Tax (BTT) to their bill. Hotel reccommndations outside the Colombo area are mentioned in the *Excursions* section of this book.

Triton Hotel

Five-Star Hotels in Colombo

CEYLON INTERCONTINENTAL
Janadhipathi Mawatha, Colombo 1
Tel: 421221
The Intercon was the first five-star hotel to be built in Sri Lanka in 1973. It overlooks the Indian Ocean at one end of Galle Face Green. Its 250 rooms have recently been refurbished.

COLOMBO HILTON
Lotus Road, Colombo 1
Tel: 544644
The newest of the island's five-star hotels, the 400-room hotel's restaurants include a pond-side coffee shop, street hawker stalls and an evening Italian outlet called the Il Ponte. The setting of the swimming pool and sports complex beside the Beira Lake compensates for its position across the road.

LANKA OBEROI
Steuart Place, Galle Road, Colombo 3
Tel: 421171
Erected in 1975, this was the second five-star hotel built on the island. The Oberoi is one of the best properties with a lovely setting and a pool in a vast expanse of garden. The lobby, built in the grand Polonnaruwa style, has a raised dais resembling the king's court, hung with 9-floor-high batiks.

THE MARRIOT
Lotus Road, Colombo 1
Tel: 544544
With a charm of its own, the 500-room Marriot (formerly the Meridien) has peaceful lobby with cascading waterfalls and greenery. There is a popular Pizza Parlour and the swimming pool is perched on the first floor, overlooking the Indian Ocean and the Presidential Secretariat.

RENAISSANCE
Sir Chittampalam Gardiner Mawatha, Colombo 2
Tel: 544200
This 357-room hotel with beautiful Sri Lanka granite floors and Kabok stones, borders the Beira Lake.

TAJ SAMUDRA
Galle Face, Colombo 3
Tel: 446622
This 400-room property, with unusual lobby decor and light fixtures designed like the inside of a Sinhala ancestral home *(walawwa)*, was the main residential venue for the SAARC in 1992. The swimming pool is at the rear, surrounded by a beautifully laid out garden.

Other Colombo hotels

GALLE FACE
2 Kollupitiya Road, Colombo 3
Tel: 541010
One of the oldest hotels in Asia. First established in 1864, the Galle Face Hotel is the only seaside hotel in the heart of Colombo where the waves roll right up to the swimming pool. Room rates start from US$35.

RENUKA
328 Galle Road, Colombo 3
Tel: 573598
A small and elegant 43-room hotel. Rates start from US$32.

MOUNT LAVINIA
Hotel Road, Mount Lavinia
Tel: 715221
Former 1810 residence of a former British Governor. There are beautiful views from the terrace of the adjoining famous Mount Lavinia beach. Rates start from US$55.

HEALTH AND EMERGENCIES

Hygiene
Except in reputed hotels, water and salads are best avoided. Drink only bottled table water or soda. Stick to fruits which can be washed and peeled. Cut fruits sold by street vendors should be avoided. Carry Lomotil tablets with you in case you come down with diarrhoea.

Beachside accommodation at the Mount Lavinia Hotel

consultation with a specialist costs under US$3, as does a routine visit to a dentist.

Hospitals

In case of an accident in Colombo, go to the Accident Service (Tel: 691111) of the General Hospital at Regent Street, Colombo 7.

There are a number of reliable private hospitals in Colombo which also offer outpatient services. Nawaloka Hospital at 23 Saugathodaya Mawatha, Colombo 2, Tel: 546258, and Durdan's Hospital at 3 Alfred Place, Colombo 3, Tel: 575205, are recommended.

COMMUNICATIONS AND NEWS

Postal Services

Your hotel will post letters for you and the mail service is quite efficient. If you are sending any valuables by post, registration is essential. The main post office is the General Post Office (Tel: 323140, open 24 hours daily).

Other post offices in Colombo are Cinnamon Gardens, Kollupitiya (Tel: 573160, open 7am–7pm Monday–Friday, 9am–7pm Saturday and 8am–10pm Sunday and public holidays), and Wellawatte (Tel: 588652, open 7am–6pm Monday–Saturday, 8am–10pm Sunday and public holidays).

Pharmacies

Most well known medicines from the West are available. The Osusala pharmacy near the Colombo Town Hall (Tel: 694716), is open 24 hours a day. There are other Osusala pharmacies throughout the island. Check with your hotel or the telephone directory for addresses

Clinics

If you want a medical check up, Colombo is one of the cheapest places to arrange one. A thorough check with all the tests costs under US$25 at Asiri Hospital, 181 Kirula Road, Colombo 5, Tel: 588267. A

Telephone

All the major hotels have International Direct Dial (IDD) facilities. For IDD enquiries dial 549215. US telephone charge cards are not yet in use here. Sri Lanka's country code is 94 and the Colombo area code is 1.

Media

There are two daily English morning newspapers, the official *Daily News* and the private *Island*, and one afternoon paper, the state-controlled *Observer*. There are three English language papers on Sundays, the state-controlled *Sunday Observer*, and the privately-run *Sunday Times* and *Sunday Island*.

Foreign newspapers such as the *International Herald Tribune*, the *Asian Wall Street Journal* and *USA Today* are available a day later at most hotel bookshops and at the sole importers, Vijitha Yapa Bookshop at 376 Galle Road, Colombo 3, Tel: 502386. Most major international publications are also available.

Two broadcast media and television stations are state controlled at present. Television begins with a 2-hour programme from 5.30am to 7.30am and then regular transmission from 4.30pm for about 6 hours. Popular Western programmes are shown on the four television channels, Rupavahini, ITN, TNL and MTV, the latter two being private stations. English television news is at 9.30pm on Rupavahini. Check the TV programme guide for CNN and BBC news times.

On radio, local English news bulletins are at 6.45am, 1.15pm, 6.15pm and 8.45pm. A short wave radio is recommended to listeners of BBC World Service.

USEFUL INFORMATION

Tourist Offices

The Ceylon Tourist Board has a travel information centre at their office at 78 Stuart Place, Colombo 3, Tel: 437059, 437060. The office is open on weekdays 8.30am–4.45pm, including *Poya* (Buddhist holidays). On Saturday, Sunday and public holidays, it is open till 12.30pm. There is also a counter in the arrival lounge of the airport.

Bookshops

There are a number of good bookshops in Colombo with a good selection of books on Sri Lanka. These include **Lake House Bookshop** on Sir Chittampalam Gardiner Mawatha, virtually opposite the Renaissance Hotel, Tel: 432104; **McCallum Book Depot** at 77 Olcott Mawatha, opposite the Fort Railway Station, Tel: 320611; **K V G de Silva** at YMBA Building, Fort and at 415 Galle Road, Colombo 4, Tel: 584146; **C Subasinghe** at Hotel Taprobane, Tel: 320391; and **Vijitha Yapa Bookshops** at three locations: 376 Galle Road, Colombo 3, Tel: 502386, 9 Kotugodella Veediya, Kandy, and at Selaka Bldg, 34 Gamini Mawatha, Galle.

Insight Guide Sri Lanka (APA Publications) and *Sri Lanka: A Travel Survival Kit* by Tony Wheeler are widely available. *Explore Sri Lanka* is a free monthly magazine for tourists, with good, reliable information.

SPORTS

Five-star hotels have swimming pools, tennis, and sports complexes including gymnasiums and health clubs. Virtually all beach resorts have pools.

Sri Lanka is a member of the International Cricket Conference. Test Matches are played with leading countries. Temporary membership is available at most cricket clubs in Colombo. The Colombo Cricket Club at 31 Maitland Crescent, Colombo 7, Tel: 691025, is recommended.

The 18-hole golf course at Nuwara Eliya, Tel: 052-3833, offers temporary membership to tourists.

For rowing enthusiasts, temporary membership is available at Colombo Rowing Club, 51/1 Sir Chittampalam Gardiner Mawatha, Colombo 2, Tel: 433758.

Underwater Safaris Ltd, 25 Barnes Place, Colombo 7, Tel: 694012, have wreck and reef diving expeditions at Hikkaduwa on the south coast.

Watersports ranging from windsurfing to skiing are available at a number of hotels in Bentota and Kalutara on the south coast and Negombo on the west coast.

USEFUL ADDRESSES

Key Telephone Numbers

Police Emergency	433333
Fire and Ambulance	422222
Accident Service	691111
Colombo General Hospital	691111
Directory Inquiries	161
Trunk Call Inquiries	161
International Inquiries	134
International Bookings	100
IDD Inquiries	549215

Credit Card Offices

AMERICAN EXPRESS
4 Leyden Bastian Road, Colombo 1
Tel: 329881

MASTERCARD
Card Centre, 90 Chatham Street,
Colombo 2
Tel: 434147

VISA
75 Bank of Ceylon Mawatha, Colombo 1
Tel: 448203

International Organisations

ALLIANCE FRANÇAISE DE COLOMBO
11 Barnes Place, Colombo 7
Tel: 694162

AMERICAN CENTER
44 Galle Road, Colombo 3
Tel: 421271-5

BRITISH COUNCIL
49 Alfred House Gardens, Colombo 7
Tel: 581171

GERMAN CULTURAL INSTITUTE
39 Gregorys Road, Colombo 7
Tel: 694562

SOVIET CULTURAL CENTRE
10 Independence Avenue, Colombo 7
Tel: 685429

UNITED NATIONS
202 Bauddhaloka Mawatha, Colombo 7
Tel: 580691

Airlines

AIRLANKA
37 York Street, Colombo 1
Tel: (Ticketing) 581131, (Reconfirmation and Reservations) 421161, (Flight Information) 446175

AEROFLOT
81 Hemas Building, Colombo 1
Tel: 325580

AIR CANADA
65 Chatham Street, Colombo 1
Tel: 540283

AIR INDIA
108 YMBA Building, Colombo 1
Tel: 325832

BRITISH AIRWAYS
c/o Renaissance Hotel, Colombo 2
Tel: 320231

CATHAY PACIFIC
186 Vauxhall Street, Colombo 1
Tel: 421931

CZECHOSLOVAKIAN AIRLINES
65 Chatham Street, Colombo 1
Tel: 548409

EMIRATES
c/o Marriot Hotel, Colombo 1
Tel: 540709

GULF AIR
Mackinons Building, Colombo 1
Tel: 326633

INDIAN AIRLINES
95 Gafoor Building, Colombo 1
Tel: 323136

JAPAN AIRLINES
c/o Marriot Hotel, Colombo 1
Tel: 541291

KLM
67 Dharmapala Mawatha, Colombo 7
Tel: 326359

KOREAN AIR
c/o Renaissance Hotel, Colombo 2
Tel: 422686

KUWAIT AIRWAYS
69 Ceylinco House, Colombo 1
Tel: 445531

LTU
11A York Street, Colombo 1
Tel: 422903

MALAYSIA AIRLINES
51 Janadhipathi Mawatha, Colombo 1
Tel: 445410

NORTHWEST
c/o Taj Samudra Hotel, Colombo 3
Tel: 446622

PIA
342 Galle Road, Colombo 3
Tel: 573475

QANTAS
5 Upper Chatham Street, Colombo 1
Tel: 435406

SAUDIA
51 Janadhipathi Mawatha, Colombo 1
Tel: 436725

SINGAPORE AIRLINES
c/o Colombo Hilton Hotel, Colombo 1
Tel: 422711

SWISSAIR
5th floor, 41 Janadhipathi Mawatha,
Colombo 1
Tel: 435403

THAI INTERNATIONAL
c/o Hotel Ceylon Intercontinental,
Colombo 1
Tel: 438050

TWA
51 Janadhipathi Mawatha, Colombo 1
Tel: 449994

Travel Agencies

A BAUR & CO
5 Upper Chatham Street, Colombo 1
Tel: 320551

AITKEN SPENCE TRAVELS
Lloyds Building, Colombo 1
Tel: 327865

ANDREWS TRAVELS
259 Duplication Road, Colombo 3
Tel: 574166

ANGLO ASIAN TRAVELS
95 Hyde Park Corner, Colombo 2
Tel: 687005

CEYLON CARRIERS LTD
104 Nawala Road, Colombo 5
Tel: 589960

CEYLON CARRIERS TRAVEL SERVICES
20 York Street, Colombo 1
Tel: 433908

CEYLON TOURS
67 Parsons Road, Colombo 2
Tel: 433404

GABO TRAVELS
59 Chatham Street, Colombo 1
Tel: 447920

GEMINI TOURS LTD
32 Queens Road, Colombo 3
Tel: 583018, 502467

GEORGE STEUARTS TRAVELS
45 Janadhipathi Mawatha, Colombo 1
Tel: 326411

HEMTOURS
24 Sir Ernest de Silva Mawatha,
Colombo 3
Tel: 575299

MACKINNONS TRAVELS
4 Leyden Bastian Road, Colombo 1
Tel: 329881

QUICKSHAWS TOURS
8 York Street, Colombo 1
Tel: 328411

SERENDIB TOURING
AA Building, Colombo 3
Tel: 433268

SPARKLINK TRAVELS
39 St Michaels Road, Colombo
Tel: 326709

UPALI TRAVELS
34 Galle Road, Colombo 3
Tel: 329399

VIP TOURS
57A Dharmapala Mawatha, Colombo 3
Tel: 448167

Foreign Missions

AUSTRALIA
3 Cambridge Place, Colombo 3
Tel: 698767

BANGLADESH
286 Bauddhaloka Mawatha, Colombo 7
Tel: 502198

BRITAIN
190 Galle Road, Colombo 3
Tel: 437336

CANADA
6 Gregorys Road, Colombo 7
Tel: 695841

CHINA
381A Bauddhaloka Mawatha, Colombo 7
Tel: 694491

EGYPT
39 Dickmans Road, Colombo 5
Tel: 583621

FINLAND
81 Barnes Place, Colombo 7
Tel: 698819

FRANCE
89 Rosmead Place, Colombo 7
Tel: 698815

GERMANY
40 Alfred House Avenue, Colombo 7
Tel: 580431

INDIA
36 Galle Road, Colombo 3
Tel: 421605

INDONESIA
1 Police Park Terrace, Colombo 5
Tel: 580113

IRAN
17 Bullers Lane, Colombo 7
Tel: 501137

IRAQ
19 Barnes Place, Colombo 7
Tel: 696600

ITALY
55 Jawatte Road, Colombo 5
Tel: 508418

JAPAN
20 Gregorys Road, Colombo 7
Tel: 693831

KOREA
98 Dharmapala Mawatha, Colombo 7
Tel: 699036

LIBYA
120 Horton Place, Colombo 7
Tel: 697311

MALAYSIA
47/1 Jawatte Road, Colombo 5
Tel: 585813

MALDIVES
25 Melbourne Avenue, Colombo 4
Tel: 586762

MYANMAR
17 Skeleton Road, Colombo 5
Tel: 587607

NETHERLANDS
25 Torrington Avenue, Colombo 7
Tel: 589626

NORWAY
34 Ward Place, Colombo 7
Tel: 692263

PAKISTAN
211 de Saram Place, Colombo 10
Tel: 696301

PALESTINE
5 Independence Avenue, Colombo 7
Tel: 695991

POLAND
120 Park Road, Colombo 5
Tel: 581903

RUSSIA
62 Sir Ernest de Silva Mawatha,
Colombo 7
Tel: 573555

SWEDEN
315 Vauxhall Street, Colombo 2
Tel: 435870

SWITZERLAND
63 Gregory's Road, Colombo 7
Tel: 695117

THAILAND
43 Dr C W Kannangara Mawatha,
Colombo 7
Tel: 697406

USA
210 Galle Road, Colombo 3
Tel: 448007

ACKNOWLEDGMENTS

Cover	**GP Reichelt/APA Photo**
Backcover	**Dallas & John Heaton/APA Photo**
Photography	**Dominic Sansoni** *and*
Pages 28, 30, 32, 35TR, 43, 45, 48B, 50, 51, 52, 54T, 55, 57, 58T, 62B, 63T, 68B, 69, 71, 74, 75B	**Vijitha Yapa**
10/11, 78, 79	**Roland Ammon/APA Photo**
46, 48T, 61	**Dallas & John Heaton/APA Photo**
40, 65,68T	**G P Reichelt/APA Photo**
24B, 59, 82B, 85	**Hans Höfer**
5	**Jean Kugler/APA Photo**
16T	**The Senanayake Family Collection**
18	**Manfred Gottschalk/APA Photo**
34B	**Philip Little/APA Photo**
37	**Alain Evrard/APA Photo**
38	**Tom Tidball**
39	**Ben Nakayama/APA Photo**
41	**Jean-Leo Dugast/APA Photo**
49	**Rainer Krack/APA Photo**
Desktop Operator	**Caroline Low**
Cover Design	**Klaus Geisler**
Cartography	**Berndtson & Berndtson**
Handwriting	**V Barl**

Index

INSIGHT *POCKET* GUIDES

• •
United States: **Houghton Mifflin Company, Boston MA 02108**
Tel: (800) 2253362 Fax: (800) 4589501

Canada: **Thomas Allen & Son, 390 Steelcase Road East**
Markham, Ontario L3R 1G2
Tel: (416) 4759126 Fax: (416) 4756747

Great Britain: **GeoCenter UK, Hampshire RG22 4BJ**
Tel: (256) 817987 Fax: (256) 817988

Worldwide: **Höfer Communications Singapore 2262**
Tel: (65) 8612755 Fax: (65) 8616438

"" I was first drawn to the Insight Guides by the excellent "Nepal" volume. I can think of no book which so effectively captures the essence of a country. Out of these pages leaped the Nepal I know – the captivating charm of a people and their culture. I've since discovered and enjoyed the entire Insight Guide Series. Each volume deals with a country or city in the same sensitive depth, which is nowhere more evident than in the superb photography. ""

Sir Edmund Hillary

INSIGHT GUIDES

COLORSET NUMBERS

You'll find the colorset number on the spine of each Insight Guide.